Industrial Espionage

Developing a Counterespionage Program

Industrial Espionage

Developing a Counterespionage Program

Daniel J. Benny, Ph.D.

CRC Press
Taylor & Francis Group
Boca Raton London New York

CRC Press is an imprint of the
Taylor & Francis Group, an **informa** business

CRC Press
Taylor & Francis Group
6000 Broken Sound Parkway NW, Suite 300
Boca Raton, FL 33487-2742

Printed on acid-free paper
Version Date: 20130725

International Standard Book Number-13: 978-1-4665-6814-3 (Hardback)

Visit the Taylor & Francis Web site at
http://www.taylorandfrancis.com

and the CRC Press Web site at
http://www.crcpress.com

This book is dedicated to

Sherlock

Winston

Mollie

Contents

Acknowledgments

Association of Former Intelligence Officers
Business Espionage Controls and Countermeasures Association
Embry-Riddle Aeronautical University
International Spy Museum
Naval Intelligence Professionals
Planehook Aviation Services, LLC
David Hook
Sherlock Holmes

I wish to thank the United Network Command for Law Enforcement without whose assistance this book would not have been possible.

About the Author

Daniel J. Benny, PhD, CPP, PCI, CFE, CCO, is a licensed private investigator and security consultant. He holds a PhD in criminal justice from Capella University, a master's degree in aeronautical science from Embry-Riddle Aeronautical University, an MA in security administration from Vermont College of Norwich University, a BA in security administration from Alvernia College, an associate's degree in arts in both commercial security and police administration from Harrisburg Area Community College; and a diploma in naval command and staff from the United States Naval War College.

He is board certified by ASIS International in security management as a certified protection professional (CPP) and as a professional certified investigator (PCI), a certified fraud examiner (CFE) by the Association of Certified Fraud Examiners, and a certified confidentiality officer (CCO) by Business Espionage Controls and Countermeasures Association.

He is the author of the books *General Aviation Security: Aircraft, Hangars, Fixed Base Operators, Flight Schools and Airports*, and *Industrial Espionage: Developing a Counterespionage Program*. He is also coauthor of the book *The Complete Guide to Physical Security*. All were published by CRC Press. He has authored more than 300 articles on security administration, intelligence, aviation security, private investigation, and cultural property security topics.

Dr. Benny served as a U. S. Naval intelligence officer with duty at the Office of Naval Intelligence, Naval Criminal Investigative Service, Willow Grove Naval Air Station, Fleet Rapid Support Team and Central Intelligence Agency. He also served as director of protective services for the Pennsylvania Historic and Museum Commission and a U.S. Navy police chief.

1

INDUSTRIAL ESPIONAGE

Motives and Threats Industrial Espionage Defined

"Espionage is not a game; it's a struggle we must win if we are to protect our freedom and our way of life." These words spoken by President Ronald Reagan during a November 30, 1985 radio speech have never been more relevant. In the world of corporate espionage, foreign intelligence, and terrorism, the struggle is never over.

Espionage is the world's second oldest profession. Industrial espionage is the theft of trade secrets by the removal, copying, or recording by technical surveillance of a company's confidential or protected information for use by a competitor or foreign nation. The protected information may include trade secrets, client lists, and other non-public information. If a company is working under a US government contract that involves US classified information at a company's facility, then that may be the target of industrial espionage.

According to the Federal Bureau of Investigation espionage is: (1) whoever knowingly performs targeting or acquisition of trade secrets to (2) knowingly benefit any foreign government, foreign instrumentality, or foreign agent. *(Title 18 U.S.C., Section 1831).*

The Federal Bureau of Investigation defines trade secrets and theft of trade secrets as: Trade secrets are all forms and types of financial, business, scientific, technical, economic or engineering information including patterns, plans, compilations, program devices, formulas, designs, prototypes, methods, techniques, processes, procedures, programs, or codes whether tangible or intangible, and whether or how stored, compiled, or memorialized physically, electronically, graphically, photographically or in writing, which the owner has taken reasonable measures to protect; and have an independent economic value. "Trade secrets" are commonly called classified proprietary

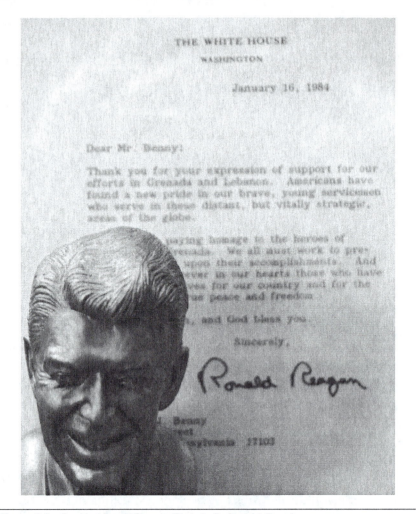

Figure 1.1   President Ronald Reagan. (Photo by Dr. Daniel J. Benny)

information, economic policy information, trade information, proprietary technology, or critical technology.

Theft of trade secrets occurs when someone (1) knowingly performs targeting or acquisition of trade secrets or intends to convert a trade secret to (2) knowingly benefit anyone other than the owner. Commonly referred to as industrial espionage. (*Title 18 U.S.C., Section 1832*).

Industrial espionage must not be confused with or compared to competitive intelligence. Competitive intelligence is the legal and ethical activity of systematically gathering, analyzing, and managing information on industrial competitors. This is non-protected information that is collected from open sources such as organizations' websites, news articles, information presented at trade shows, or company brochures. Competitive intelligence may also include information obtained from public filings such as property records and permits.

As previously stated, industrial espionage is not only unethical, but is also a criminal offense under all state criminal statutes and federal law. Over the years, there have been a series of serious industrial espionage cases. One case involved the Avery Dennison Corp, a major United States adhesives company, in which company secrets were stolen and sold to Four Pillars, a Taiwanese company that also makes and sells pressure-sensitive products.

Another case of corporate espionage was dubbed "Japscam" by the press. Hitachi came into possession of an almost full set of IBM's Adirondack Workbooks. The workbooks contained IBM design documents and technical secrets that were prominently marked FOR INTERNAL IBM USE ONLY. Hitachi did not return them to IBM.

Gillette had a close shave with industrial espionage when company secrets were stolen and offered for sale to a company in the same market. The company reported the attempt to Gillette and an arrest was made of the individual.

The following history of espionage legislation in the United States demonstrates the attempt to reduce the threat from industrial espionage.

US Espionage Acts of 1917

The US Espionage Act of 1917 was passed to protect the United States during a time of war and made it a criminal offense to pass on information with intent to interfere with the operation or success of the armed forces of the United States or to aid the enemies of the United States. Theses offenses were punishable by death or by imprisonment for not more than thirty years or both. Under the US Espionage Act of 1917, it was also an offense to convey false reports or false statements with intent to interfere with the operation or success of the military or naval forces of the United States. This also included the promotion of enemies of the United States when the country is at war and to cause or attempt to cause insubordination, disloyalty, mutiny, refusal of duty, in the military or naval forces of the United States, or to willfully obstruct the recruiting or enlistment service of the United

States. These offenses were punishable by a maximum fine of $10,000 or by imprisonment for not more than twenty years or both.

While the Espionage Act of 1917 dealt with espionage and subversion against the United States, it did little to provide for the prevention and prosecution of individuals taking part in industrial espionage against private industries. (See Appendix A.)

The US Economic Espionage Act of 1996

The US Economic Espionage Act of 1996 was passed into law to provide for the prosecution of individuals taking part in industrial or economic espionage and the theft of trade secrets that would benefit any foreign government, foreign instrument, or foreign agent. The law specifically addresses trade secrets.

An important aspect of the Economic Espionage Act of 1996 was that it not only allowed for the prosecution of the perpetrators, but it also allowed the targeted company to seek financial reimbursement for losses the organization suffered as a direct result of the theft of trade secrets. This aspect of the law also holds responsible the organization that facilitated, or would have gained from, the industrial espionage and trade secrets stolen from the targeted company. (See Appendix B.)

Uniform Trade Secrets Act

The federal espionage laws deal with the protection of US government's interests and espionage perpetrated by foreign government, businesses, and agents. To resolve this situation, the Uniform Trade Secrets Act, published by the Uniform Law Commission in 1979 and later amended in 1985, has the goal of providing a uniform act as a legal framework for trade secrets protection for the private industry within the United States of America. The Uniform Trade Secrets Act aimed to codify standards and remedies regarding the misappropriation of trade secrets that emerged in common law on a state-to-state basis. (See Appendix C.)

State Laws Related to Trade Secrets and Espionage

In order to provide for the prosecution of private individuals and organizations without foreign influence, most states have passed industrial espionage laws. Depending on the state where one is located, that state's laws need to be examined.

US Intelligence Agencies

The United States intelligence community consists of the following agencies:

Director of National Intelligence
Central Intelligence Agency
National Security Agency/Central Security Service
National Reconnaissance Office
National Geospatial Intelligence Agency
Defense Security Service
Defense Intelligence Agency
Federal Bureau of Investigation
Department of Homeland Security Office of Intelligence and Analysis
United States Army Intelligence and Security Command
Office of Naval Intelligence
Marine Corps Intelligence
United States Air Force Air Intelligence Agency
Drug Enforcement Administration
State Department Intelligence
Treasury Department Office of Intelligence Support

Theoretically, it is possible that a private organization facing the threat of or being a victim of industrial espionage may have contact with any of these agencies, especially if the company is involved with a government classified contract. Most often, the only agency a company would interact with would be the Federal Bureau of Investigation.

Federal Bureau of Investigation (FBI)

The Federal Bureau of Investigation is the primary federal law enforcement agency responsible for the investigation of espionage in the United States. The FBI Directorate of Intelligence manages all FBI intelligence activities and works with all bureau offices, making certain that intelligence is embedded in every investigative program and field office. They would be contacted on any industrial espionage case.

Department of Homeland Security Office of Intelligence and Analysis

Protecting the American people from terrorist threats is the founding purpose of this department and its highest priority. The Department's efforts in battling terrorism, helping protect transportation and critical infrastructure and cyber networks from attack, detecting agents of biological warfare, and building information-sharing partnerships with state and local law enforcement can enable law enforcement to mitigate threats. This agency is contacted if it is believed that some form of transportation is being used for the theft of protected information.

State Department Intelligence

The intelligence function of the State Department concerns the protection of embassies, diplomatic staffs, and foreign visitors to the United States. The intelligence also focuses on foreign affairs that could impact critical Department of State decisions. This organization provides excellent training material to brief employees on counterespionage when traveling overseas.

Treasury Department Office of Intelligence Support

The focus of the Treasury Department Office of Intelligence Support is the tracking of money used in terrorism, espionage, and organized crime. The Treasury Department also explores organizations that might be used as front groups to launder money for criminal and terrorist activity. If there is evidence a company's financial department is being used for espionage, the Treasury Department may be called in to assist.

Defense Security Service

The Defense Security Service (DSS) is a division of the Department of Defense (DoD). The DSS is located in Quantico, Virginia with field offices throughout the United States. The Under Secretary of Defense for Intelligence provides authority, direction, and control over DSS. DSS provides the military services, defense agencies, twenty-four federal agencies and approximately 13,300 cleared contractor facilities, private industry, and universities with security support services.

Determining the Value of Information

Industrial espionage is not just the loss of protected information that may be used by another organization or foreign government. While it is not a physical asset such as a company vehicle, aircraft, or building, nonetheless, information, especially in industry, has a monetary value. It represents the time invested in the creation of the documents, the price someone would pay for that information or those documents, or the loss of revenue an organization would suffer if a rival organization were able to bring a new product to the market because of industrial espionage.

In determining the value of protected information, a company must look at the investment in the time and research that went into gathering and/or creating the information. This includes capital spent, salaries of individuals who work on the project, plus the cost of storing and securing the information. The company must also evaluate the replacement cost to the organization, if possible. The final area to consider is the monetary loss if the information were to be used by another organization.

When considering the threat of industrial espionage, it is not just the security of protected information that must be considered. In the threat evaluation, the value and the impact on the company of the loss of such information must also be considered.

Figure 1.2   The International Spy Museum in Washington, D.C. has one of the most comprehensive collections of books and DVDs covering the history of espionage, espionage tradecraft, current events, and intelligence community in the world. (Photo by Dr. Daniel J. Benny)

Conditions for Industrial Espionage

Five conditions contribute to the successful completion of industrial espionage:

Motive
Opportunity
Rationalization
Ability
Trigger

Motive

In order to successfully counter industrial espionage, it is critical to have an understanding of the motives of individuals who take part in such deceptive and criminal activity. While the individual motives may vary, there is a commonality that surrounds the act of bringing the act of industrial espionage to fruition. The motive may be monetary, revenge, or a religious, political, or social view. It may be simply for the thrill. In any event, the most common motive is money.

Opportunity

Opportunity is the circumstance in which an individual has access to protected information and feels that he or she can steal or reproduce the information without detection or consequences. Ultimately, if there is an opportunity for industrial espionage, the security is inadequate. This inadequate security may be due to insufficient physical security such as a lack of barriers, access control, intrusion detection systems, security cameras, security containers, and/or security officers. When there is an opportunity for industrial espionage it is more often a more systemic issue rather than just a lack of physical security.

A lack of policy, internal controls, supervision, training, and audits creates an atmosphere where individuals have access to protected information. This lack leads these individuals to feel that they can steal without detection and consequences. When a security breach occurs and is not followed by an adequate investigation and disciplinary action against the offender, those who seek to take part in espionage will be emboldened.

Rationalization

Rationalization is ability of the perpetrators of espionage to justify to themselves why the industrial espionage is not really wrong. This justification may conclude that it was for a good cause because it supports their political or ideological views. Other justifications may be that everyone else does it or that the perpetrator did not get a raise. If the espionage is done for money, the rationalization may be that the company can afford the loss.

Ability

Ability in this instance means that to take part in criminal behaviors such as industrial espionage, the person is able to overcome natural inhibitors. The person must put aside moral values, loyalty to the nation or employer, and most of all the fear of being discovered.

Trigger

Many things can trigger the betrayal that causes an individual to take part in industrial espionage. An individual may take part in espionage to obtain additional funds; but in most cases, the primary pressure is the desperate need for money. An individual may need funds to support an extravagant lifestyle, or an addiction to drug, alcohol, or gambling. It may also be related to sexual activity wherein an individual is being exploited and takes part in espionage for a lover or an individual may be the subject of blackmail. Pressure may also be related to membership in criminal, terrorist, or ideological groups that seek protected information that the perpetrator may have access to.

These conditions provide the basis for the recruitment of individuals including employees of organizations targeted by foreign governments and competitors.

Espionage Threat from Foreign Governments   Foreign governments are a serious threat in perpetrating industrial espionage in their attempts to obtain information about adversary countries. The stolen information is used to aid the offending country's economic development, to gain a competitive edge, or to promote its own domestic agenda. The open source and protected information these governments seek is varied and includes military capabilities, weapons systems, communications, industrial processes, clean-energy, technical and scientific technology, location of natural resources, and virtually any sensitive information related to the target country.

While governmental agencies are the targets of such espionage, private corporations and education institution are also targeted. These entities conduct the research and produce the products and processes sought by foreign nations. It is because of this industrial espionage threat to private industry that an effective counterespionage program is essential not only to the security of the target company, but also to the national security of the country in which it is located.

The primary and most serious threats from foreign nations to the United States, United Kingdom, Canada, European countries, and Israel are from China, Russia, and Iran. In a November 3, 2011 report on espionage to Congress, the Office of the National

Counterintelligence Executive named China as the world's most active and persistent perpetrator of economic espionage against United States private sector companies. Russian was named the second most serious threat to protected information. As will be discussed later in this book, the Internet and the increased use of technology devices have made it easy for foreign entities such as China and Russia to collect enormous quantities of data quickly and with little risk.

As stated by the US Office of National Counterintelligence:

> In 2010, the FBI prosecuted more Chinese espionage cases than at any time in our nation's history. Although cyber intrusions linked to China have received considerable media attention, some of the most damaging transfers of US technologies to foreign entities have been conducted by insiders. For example, a DuPont chemist in October 2010 pled guilty to stealing research from the company on organic light-emitting diodes, which the chemist intended to commercialize in China with financial help from the Chinese government.
>
> Similarly, the unmasking of the network of ten Russian "illegals" implanted on American soil indicated that these spies had been tasked to collect data on economic as well as political and military issues.

The third most serious threat is from Iran and the terrorist organizations that Iran utilizes and supports globally in the spread of Jihadist Islamic views. This is accomplished by organizations such as the Muslim Brotherhood and their front groups. While China, Russia, and Iran are the most serious threats related to industrial espionage, a threat can come from almost any country including so-called friendly nations. It is for this reason that all organizations with vital information must stay vigilant. Trust no one.

Espionage Threat from Competitors   The threat from competitors to private industry organization is substantial. This includes companies that are in the same line business be it retail, production, or research. A competitor will seek inside information to gain the competitive edge in the market. Most information obtained from competitors is collected through legal open-source collections known as competitive intelligence. Most legitimate private organizations will not take part in illegal industrial espionage. There have been many situations where an employee from an organization approached a competitor company to sell protected information and that company, in turn, reported the offender to the company for which he or she worked and also to law enforcement authorities. With that said, it is important to understand that there are unethical organizations that will steal or obtain protected information from freelance industrial espionage operatives.

An additional threat would be a foreign competitor company which is owned by the government in the country it is located. This is one method employed by China and so-called private companies operating from that country. In fact, these companies are owned by and operating under the direction of the Chinese government to steal protected information from private companies in various nations.

It is vital that the security departments of large and small corporations become aware of intelligence collecting techniques by all competitors.

Espionage Threat from Inside An employee or contractor working inside the company taking part in industrial espionage over a long period of time is the most serious threat to an organization or the nation's secrets. According to the Office of National Counterintelligence, insiders who seek to harm US security interests normally are either long-term plants or people who have been lured to betray their nation for ideological reasons, a lust for money or sex, or through blackmail. The methods may change, but core motivations do not. Insiders convicted of espionage have, on average, been active for a number of years before being caught. In addition, according to the Office of National Counterintelligence more information can be carried out the door on removable media in a matter of minutes than the sum total of what was given to our enemies in hard copy throughout the US history of espionage in both the government and private sector. Consequently, the damage caused by malicious insiders today will likely continue to increase until there are effective insider threat detection programs that can proactively identify and mitigate the threats before they fully mature.

According to Richards J. Heuer, Jr. of the Defense Personnel Security Research Center:

The initiative for most insider espionage comes from the insider, not from the foreign organization or group that receives the information. The overwhelming majority (over 79%) of Americans arrested for espionage during the past 50 years were either volunteers who took the initiative in contacting a foreign intelligence service or were recruited by an American friend or relative who had volunteered to a foreign intelligence service.

The case of former Navy Warrant Officer John Walker who provided top secret classified US Navy information to the Soviet Union for decades and caused grave damage to the United States exemplifies the serious threat from an employee.

The decision of employees to take part in industrial espionage may be for personal gain, to release protected information on the Internet for revenge, to make a political or ideological statement, or for thrill seeking.

An employee of a company may be targeted for industrial espionage by a foreign nation. This is the number one source of industrial espionage and the loss of protected information. The loss may be great because the individuals recruited have access to the information over a long period since they are employed at the target location. The employees also know the internal workings of company security procedures, and the physical security systems and how to circumvent them. By utilizing an employee for industrial espionage, the handler of that employee is subjected to less risk of identification.

FBI Warning Signs of Insider Espionage

They work odd hours without authorization.

Without need or authorization, they take proprietary or other information home in hard copy form and/or on thumb drives, computer disks, or e-mail.

They unnecessarily copy material, especially if it's proprietary or classified.

They disregard company policies about installing personal software or hardware, accessing restricted websites, conducting unauthorized searches, or downloading confidential material.

They take short trips to foreign countries for unexplained reasons.

They engage in suspicious personal contacts with competitors, business partners, or other unauthorized individuals.

They buy things they can't afford.

They are overwhelmed by life crises or career disappointments.

They are concerned about being investigated, leaving traps to detect searches of their home or office or looking for listening devices or cameras.

One of the resources offered by the FBI is InfraGard, an information sharing and analysis effort serving the interests and combining the knowledge base of a wide range of members. At its most basic level, InfraGard is a partnership between the FBI and the private sector. InfraGard is an association of individuals, academic institutions, state and local law enforcement agencies, and other participants dedicated to sharing information and intelligence to prevent hostile acts against the United States. Infragard chapters are geographically linked with FBI field office territories.

The insider threat from industrial espionage is more serious than ever. This, in part, is because of the digital age in which we now live. Years ago, insiders had to photocopy and smuggle mountains of documents out of their offices in a covert manner. Today documents can be shared via e-mail or downloaded electronically on easy-to-hide portable devices.

Espionage Threat from Freelance Industrial Espionage Operatives

In the realm of industrial espionage, freelance espionage operatives also present a threat. These individuals often have criminal records or may be former intelligence officers for a governmental intelligence service that is now operating independently. They may be hired by other individual or organizations to take part in industrial espionage.

These freelance industrial espionage operatives may, on their own accord, steal protected information and then attempt to sell that information to the highest bidder. Potential customers could be governments, organizations, companies, criminal or terrorist groups, or private individuals. Their primary motive is monetary.

In summary, adversaries of the US government and private industry throughout history have routinely threatened the information of the nation. Foreign intelligence services, criminals, private sector spies, and insiders such as employees and contractors are focused on American industry and the private sector. These adversaries use traditional intelligence tradecraft against vulnerable companies. The efforts of these predators compromise intellectual property, trade secrets, and technological developments that are critical to national security and the private companies from which such information is stolen. This espionage against the private sector increases the danger to long-term private and US prosperity.

The private sector must ensure that it has the knowledge, resources, and expertise to thwart these efforts to steal critical company information. Counterintelligence is a challenge for corporations and private industry as it can absorb company resources that would otherwise be used for growth and at a time when an understanding of the serious threat presented by industrial espionage is lacking. Private industry and corporations must develop a counterespionage plan to prevent and reduce the threat from industrial espionage.

Bibliography

Association of Certified Fraud Examiners (2000). *Corporate Espionage*. Austin, TX: Association of Certified Fraud Examiners.

Central Intelligence Agency (2012). *Factbook*. Washington, DC: US Government Printing Office.

Defense Security Service (2013). Retrieved from http://www.dss.mil/

Heuer, R. J. (2012). The insider espionage threat. Retrieved from http://rf-web.tamu.edu/security/Security%20Guide/Treason/Insider.htm

Heims, P. (1982). *Countering Industrial Espionage*. Surrey, UK: 20th Century Security Education.

Johnson, W.M. (2007). *Business Espionage*. Shoreline, WA: Questor Group.

Martin, S. (2005). *Business Intelligence and Corporate Espionage*. Boston, MA: Pearson.

The National Counterintelligence Center (2011). Annual Report to Congress on Foreign Economic Collection and Industrial Espionage. Washington, DC: U.S. Government Printing Office.

Office of National Intelligence (2013). Retrieved from http://www.intelligence.gov/about-the-intelligence-community.

Richelson, J. T. (1999). *The US Intelligence Community*. Boulder, CO: Westview Press

Winker, I. (1997). *Corporate Espionage*. New York, NY: Prima Publishing.

2

Espionage Tradecraft

Only by understanding the threats and the basics of the tradecraft utilized to facilitate industrial espionage can an organization develop an effective counterespionage program. A review of espionage tradecraft will include the intelligence cycle, the categories of intelligence collection, and the methods of collection.

The Intelligence Cycle

There are five-steps in the intelligence process called the Intelligence Cycle. This process ensures the collection process is done correctly by use of a system of checks and balances.

Planning and Direction

Planning is the first phase of the process during which the decision is made concerning what intelligence is required, the sources of the intelligence needed, how it will be collected, and the value of such information. At this stage, the target company or individual will be identified. The type of information required from the target is then decided. The methods of collection will be decided upon and the techniques of using such collection methods must also be determined.

The budget must also be determined. This will include salary of agents; cost of collection equipment to be used, travel, possible hotel cost and other expenses. The funds, if any, used to pay for information retrieved through espionage must also be considered.

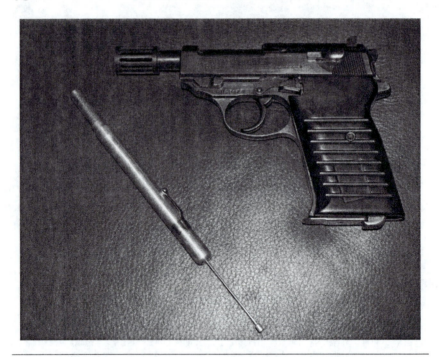

Figure 2.1   The tools used in industrial espionage tradecraft are not what one would see in the cinema such as the U.N.C.L E pistol and pen communicator. (Photo by Daniel J. Benny)

Collection

The collection phase is the gathering of intelligence information overtly (openly) and covertly (secretly). Examples of open-source information include reading foreign newspapers and magazine articles, listening to foreign radio, and watching overseas television. Other information sources may be covert (or secret), such as illegal information collected with listening devices and hidden cameras.

Processing

This phase of the intelligence cycle deals with taking all of the information collected and putting it into a usable intelligence report for the customer. The final product may be a report, photographs, video, charts, maps and graphs or a voice recording. Whatever the media chosen, it must be formatted in a form that can be used and based on what the customer requires.

Analysis and Production

During this phase, all the collected information is reviewed for quality and value and is formatted into the final product. This final written report or collection of photographs/video, charts, maps and graphs or voice recording, however the intelligence was processed, is put to use. In some situations, it may be determined at this phase that addition intelligence is required at which point the collection cycle begins again.

Dissemination

In this final phase of the cycle, the final written analysis is provided to the intelligence customer. The customer may come back with more questions. Then the whole process starts over again

Categories of Intelligence Collection and Tradecraft

Within the intelligence community there are five categories of intelligence collection. The intelligence categories are identified by the type of intelligence and how it is collected.

- Human Intelligence (HUNINT)
- Imagery Intelligence (IMINT)
- Open Source Intelligence (OSINT)
- Signals Intelligence (SIGINT)
- Measure and Signatures (MASINT)

Human Intelligence (HUNINT)

Human intelligence is derived from or collected by human sources such as agents, informants, and human assets. Human intelligence is the most common method used for industrial espionage. The reason is that an individual or asset can be recruited from the target company. This will afford the asset both the access and long period of time required to collect the targeted protected information.

Methods of Recruitment   When a foreign nation, competitor, freelance espionage operative, or terrorist organization seeks to obtain protected information from an organization, there is, of course, the requirement of access to the information they are seeking. The goal is to obtain the information covertly, without the knowledge of the organization they are stealing it from, by photographing, photocopying, downloading the protected information from a computer system or transmitting it electronically while leaving the original source of the information intact. In this way, the target organization will not realize that information is being stolen thus allowing the perpetrator to continue the industrial espionage indefinitely and often for many years.

The country, organization, or individual seeking such information can attempt to infiltrate the target company. Not being an employee with approved access, it is not be easy to infiltrate the company in most cases. Human intelligence collection may also include the use of pretexts to gain information from individuals by phone, e-mail, or in person. A pretext may also be used to gain access into a targeted organization. The pretext may be appearing as a customer, a public utilities inspector, a delivery person, or a building inspector.

Covert entry is possible, but if successful, it only allows one time access to the protected information. Obtaining employment for the purpose of espionage will allow long term access. To obtain employment, there must be an opening and the organization agent who will carry out the espionage must meet the position's requirement, pass security investigations, and be hired. This is not always achievable and if the person does obtain the position, it can take considerable time before he or she has access to the desired information. The agent must also study and work around the security program that is in place in order to obtain the required information through espionage.

The most effective method of information collection would be to recruit an employee, referred to as an asset or mole, who is already working at the target organization and who has access to the protected information the organization seeks to obtain. The asset will know the security procedures and physical security systems that have been established to prevent espionage. With this knowledge, the asset can easily circumvent the security systems. By recruiting a current employee, there is the expectation of long term access to protected information, which could last for decades. Using a current employee at the target location as an asset is not only of value to the agent or handler, this method also reduces the risk to the agent or the asset handler from identification and possible arrest for industrial espionage.

The recruitment of an asset can take time, but if successful, can result in the collection of an enormous amount of information over many years. The goal of the recruitment process is to find the right asset within the targeted company. When selecting an asset, there are several primary methods of recruitment to secure the asset's cooperation.

Most cases of industrial espionage where human intelligence is utilized involve the asset's desire for monetary gain. This need for money may just be to live a more enjoyable lifestyle. It may be to pay for expensive habits or addictions such as drugs, alcohol, gambling, sex, or just the need to buy things. It may also may be due to health issues wherein the asset needs money to pay medical bills or routine bills and credit cards. If may also be due to divorce actions and the need to make payment to the former spouse and legal fees.

To recruit these employees as assets, the handler will gather intelligence on the various employees of a company to identify those in need of money due to debt, divorce actions, addictions or medical issues. This information may be obtained by searching public records of divorces or bankruptcy filings. Other methods might include frequenting restaurants where employees of the target company gather and to listen and to get to know individuals. A particular individual may be targeted based on his or her position in the target company.

Once a possible asset is identified, the handler will befriend the asset, get to know him or her and at some point will offer to help resolve the situation by offering extra money for information. Initially, the information requested may seem innocent such as an employee directory. The handler will gradually upgrade the information requested as he or she continues to pay for information.

Should the asset desire to discontinue stealing and providing the protected information requested, the handler will attempt to blackmail the asset. In most cases, the handler will document the transfer of protected document and payment with photographs or recordings. If the asset at some point in time wishes to discontinue the espionage, the handler will then expose this evidence and threaten to tell the asset's employer or even law enforcement about the theft of the protected or classified company information. In some situations, an individual will approach an intelligence agency, criminal or terrorists group and offer to conduct espionage for them.

Blackmail can also be used as the initial method to recruit an asset. The handler will arrange placing the prospective asset in a compromising position and document it. Most often this is a sexual compromise called a honey trap. If the target asset is married then there is the threat to turn over documentation of the discretion to the spouse. The sexual activity may also be homosexual or other activity such as bondage. The evidence of the compromising situation, no matter what it may be, will then be used as the leverage for blackmail in return for conducting espionage.

In some cases an individual's ideological or religious views may be used to turn the individual into an asset for the cause. Such individuals may even serve as an asset without the payment of funds because it is a cause or religious view that they support. The cause may be socialism over capitalism, or it could be an environmental issue. The religious view is often used when espionage is conducted by Islamic nations or Islamic terror groups. The religion, if Islam, often encompasses all aspects of the believer's life including political, religious, and personal lifestyle. Regardless of how assets are recruited once they have stolen protected information or divulged secret information they are trapped and cannot walk away.

Once recruited, the assets receive training from their handlers on the tradecraft of espionage and the various collection methods. The asset is trained both on how to collect information and also what information is to be targeted. The most secure methods of obtaining the target information are also covered in the training.

In addition, the asset is trained on the way to contact the handler in order to pass on the information. The first step is to inform the handler that information or money needs to be picked up. The most common method is to have prearranged items identified such as a light pole, mail box, or park bench. If there is to be a pick up or drop off, place a chalk mark or tape on the item as notification of the exchange of information or money.

To accomplish the transfer, several methods are commonly utilized. One is the brush pass technique. This requires skill and coordination, but it is an effective method. Two or more agents literally brush past one another, passing the information or money from hand to hand as they go by. This may be done any number of places, but is accomplished most effectively and securely in very busy areas where there are large crowds. Variations include standing together on a busy train or passing documents between restroom stalls in a busy public washroom.

A dead drop or dead letter box can also be used in an unpopulated area at a pre-planned location. The agent loads the dead drop by placing the item for later collection by another agent or the asset, be it information or money. This method alleviates the need for the two individuals to be in the same place at the same time. Examples include hiding information or money in a soda can, under a rock or other item, or in a hollow tree.

The use of a live drop or live letter box is also common. This is similar to the dead drop except that a person is used instead of an object. For example, the agent brings his suit to the drycleaners, where a person known to the agent works. Inside his jacket will be the letter that needs to be transferred. To any surveillance watching, the agent is just dropping off laundry. Later, another agent will come in to retrieve his suits and will be given the letter by the employee, probably inside one of the suits.

Imagery Intelligence (IMINT)

Various forms of technical surveillance are employed for industrial espionage. Use of imaging techniques to collect information through industrial espionage ranges from mobile phones, cameras, professional digital cameras, or videos operated by individuals on the ground, in motor vehicles, or in small aircraft. In many industrial espionage operations where the information is collected by an agent on the ground or an asset in a targeted facility, the images may be collected with a handheld, full-size or miniature digital camera or a disguised digital camera concealed in a pen or within some other common item that an individual would normally carry.

The images collected may be existing digital photographs that have been illegally downloaded from a computer. The illegal image may be an existing photograph that can be copied on a copy machine, scanned into a computer, and downloaded or re-photographed with a camera.

The most recent technology involves the use of very small unmanned aerial vehicles or UAVs. These small airborne platforms are used in the collection of information in remote areas or where there is no visibility from the ground view or surrounding terrain. Satellites that can record images from space may be utilized if the industrial espionage is being conducted by foreign nations that have the technology to use satellite imagery for espionage collection. Imaging techniques may also be used to obtain information on a targeted item. The video camera is most often used by organizations that are gathering intelligence on a possible target location for a terrorist attack,

These techniques may also be used to document individuals, the movement of individuals, or security force operation for a terrorist attack against an individual or a facility. Imagery of a target facility may also be acquired to facilitate a clandestine entry into the target property.

Open Source Intelligence (OSINT)

As discussed under human intelligence, open source intelligence is the collection of public domain information that is legally available to anyone. Public information is not always free information. There may be a fee to access the information. The primary difference between open source information and trade secrets is that there is a public right to access of the information in some form.

The gathering of intelligence from sources available to the public such as print material, Internet, video clips, and photographs is open source collection. This is legal. Much useful intelligence can be obtained using this method with no risk to the individual collecting the information whether the asset that was recruited or an intelligence agent or handler.

Open-source information can also come from governmental organizations, trade and professional organization publications, conferences, information from the target company's own web page and publications, and trade shows. An example of a federal government source would be Securities and Exchange Commission filings which are a requirement of publicly-traded companies. Annual and quarterly reports can be obtained through this source. Information on stock holders and income statement can also be accessed.

All states require that companies doing business within their jurisdiction register, in most case with the secretary of state. Information on the target corporation, the officers and other vital information can be obtained. Plans of a target companies including their plans for expansion can be obtained from a local court house where deeds and transactions are filed.

Trade and professional organization publications such as Dun & Bradstreet and Lexis/Nexis databases can also be an open source of intelligence. Organizations provide intelligence on their company websites and social links such as Facebook, Twitter, and LinkedIn. A target organization's booth at a trade show provides an excellent opportunity to collect information about that company both from handouts being distributed and by talking with a company representative.

Special methods of open source tradecraft include observing how many trucks a company is using to move goods and the time of movements. This can give an indication as to the amount of business the company has. Dumpster diving, or going through an organization's trash can yield valuable information and is legal in most areas as long as the trash has been placed at the curb. It would be illegal to access a company's property to explore and remove their trash in most areas.

Another method is to go to a local eatery where employees of a nearby company go for breakfast, lunch or to meet after work. By sitting near the group and listening, much open source information about the company can be learned from the conversations. It is also possible to become involved in conversations and gather even more information.

Posing as a customer of a company is still another excellent method of obtaining open source information. Company representative are willing to do what it takes to please customers and will provide the customer with much information.

Signals Intelligence (SIGINT)

Signals intelligence is information derived from the interception of signals from communications, electronics, and telemetry. It is the interception of communication. This includes the use of technology to intercept oral communication, telephone communication, and e-mail communication between individuals and organizations.

SIGINT consists of:

- Communications Intelligence (COMINT)—technical and intelligence information derived from intercept of foreign communications.
- Electronic Intelligence (ELINT)—information collected from systems such as radars and other weapons systems.
- Foreign Instrumentation Signals Intelligence (FISINT)—signals detected from weapons under testing and development.

Methods of monitoring oral communication between individuals can be accomplished with the use of a parabolic microphone, microwave interception, and hard-wired or wireless microphones and transmitters. The transmitters may be FM or a spread spectrum broadband radio signal. This type of monitoring can even be accomplished with a modified mobile phone left in a targeted room. If the mobile phone is discovered, one might assume it was just left in the location by accident and not for the purpose of industrial espionage.

Such listening and transmission devices can be concealed in most any object. This is especially true if device is battery operated. If the device is hard-wired, then it will be hidden where there is access to an electric source such as a light switch or wall outlets.

The monitoring of telephone communication is a common source of information. This can be accomplished using a series wiretap that monitors one side of the phone conversation or a parallel wiretap that monitors both sides of the phone conversation. Such surveillance equipment can be positioned at numerous places along the telephone line.

The surveillance of e-mail transmission can be accomplished by use of a key logger that allows access to the target computer or by the use of spyware that allows remote access to the target computer. These and other methods will be discussed further in the text under cyber security.

Measure and Signatures (MASINT)

Measure and signatures intelligence is derived from acoustic and radiation sources. Examples of this type intelligence include information related to nuclear and sound activity from which vital information can be gained.

There are several important distinctions between MASINT and the other categories of intelligence that have been discussed. MASINT is a relatively new technology and has very diverse options for use. Many MASINT-based systems are used in a variety of roles for intelligence collection just as varied as intruder detection systems or strategic missile launch warning systems are used. MASINT-based systems for the most part are used by government military or intelligence services for the collection of protected information, battle information, or for state security matters, and counterespionage activities. An organization being targeted with MASINT, in most cases, is facing a serious and qualified espionage threat as the adversary is most likely a foreign government intelligence service seeking highly protected and classified information.

The following are included in measures and signatures collection:

- Radar Intelligence (RADINT)
- Acoustic Intelligence (ACOUSTINT)
- Nuclear Intelligence (NUCINT)
- Radio Frequency/Electromagnetic Pulse Intelligence (RF/ EMPINT)
- Electro-optical Intelligence (ELECTRO-OPTINT)
- Laser Intelligence (LASINT)
- Materials Intelligence
- Unintentional Radiation Intelligence (RINT)
- Chemical and Biological Intelligence (CBINT)
- Directed Energy Weapons Intelligence (DEWINT)
- Effluent/Debris Collection
- Spectroscopic Intelligence
- Infrared Intelligence (IRINT)

Deception and Pretext Tradecraft

In the world of industrial espionage, deception is used to obtain protected information. Most often the deception is in the form of a pretext. A pretext as it relates to industrial espionage involves assuming an identity or appearance other than one's own in order to cloak the person's real intentions which are the solicitations of protected information. Some forms of pretexts are legal as long as one is not using false identification, wearing uniforms or representing himself or herself as a law enforcement officer or a public utility employee. Even if the pretext is not illegal, depending on the how the pretext was used, civil action could result for the invasion of privacy or other damages that may have occurred.

There are many pretexts that can be used to solicit information. The primary premise of a pretext is to hide one's real identity or motives. This is often accomplished by utilizing false credentials and dressing to the part that may include the wearing of uniforms based on the nature of the pretext. Some pretext attacks require no false credential or special dress or uniforms at all.

With the capability of computer publishing and copying, the creation of totally fictitious identifications or the fraudulent reproduction of real identifications is quite easy. Digital photography photos and logos can be inserted on the false identification. The fictitious identifications that are created could be those of a public office holder, a law enforcement officer, private investigator, utility worker, news reporter or delivery worker. The identification might be a fraudulent reproduction of a company's real identification that the perpetrator wants to access.

Dressing for the part includes a fraudulent uniform of a police officer or a delivery worker from a nationally known company. Often it includes a jacket, sweatshirt or other garment with a fraudulent logo imprinted on the garment to provide the illusion that the person represents a legitimate company.

The ploys are limited only by the imagination when it comes to the use of deception and pretexts in facilitation of industrial espionage. Examples include seeking employment, writing a college paper, seeking a news story, delivery, or trying to locate a friend or business associate.

Before an individual uses a pretext for industrial espionage, he or she will conduct a background inquiry on the target or target location. If the target is a person, as much information as possible will be obtained in advance such as address, work location, vehicle driven, family members, travel routine, and routine stops during travel.

If the target is a location, the hours of operations will be identified, along with employee and visitor traffic patterns. The physical security such as security cameras, intrusion detections system and access control will be determined. The number and type security force will also be identified as well as the movements, shifts, and schedules of the security force members.

In some situations, the actual pretext attack may commence with a telephone call to the target or target company to obtain information that can be used in person at the target location. The phone call may also be used to lay the ground work for the actual visit to the target location that would make that conclusion of the pretext successful.

An example of a case of industrial espionage in which there was the use of pretext involved three individuals associated with a private investigation firm in Florida The three private investigators were found to have been using false identities to obtain the home records of board members, employees, and journalists. The employees of the private investigative firm were found guilty and have been sentenced in connection with a Hewlett-Packard spying scandal.

The private investigative firm was hired on behalf of Hewlett-Packard's CEO to probe boardroom leaks to journalists in 2005. The three private investigators used pretexting. Using false identifications and by posing as account holders or employees of various phone companies, they were able to fraudulently obtain personal information on the target group which included board members, employees, and journalists. The information that the three private investigators obtained using a pretext included phone numbers, dates of birth, social security numbers, call logs, various billing records, and detailed subscriber information. The private investigators also obtained confidential information belonging to Hewlett-Packard board members, employees and their families. They also obtained confidential information on reports for Cnet, the *Wall Street Journal,* the *New York Times*, and the journalists' families.

The investigative firm stated they used such pretext methods for years and grossed up to $30,000 just on that practice alone. Pretexting and the sale of phone records obtained using the technique led to a national controversy and congressional hearings on the subject. The Federal Communications Commission conducted its own investigation of the incident.

As stated previously. some forms of pretexting are legal; the pretext methods these investigators used were not. Their actions were also unethical and were not actions in which a professional private investigator or private investigative or security should participate.

Bibliography

Association of Certified Fraud Examiners (2000). *Corporate Espionage*. Austin, TX: Association of Certified Fraud Examiners.

Central Intelligence Agency (2012) *Factbook*. Washington, DC: U.S. Government Printing Office.

Defense Security Service (2013) Retrieved from http://www.dss.mil/

Heims, P. (1982). *Countering Industrial Espionage*. Surrey, UK: 20th Century Security Education.

Johnson, W.M. (2007). *Business Espionage*. Shoreline, WA: Questor Group

Martin, S. (2005) *Business Intelligence and Corporate Espionage*. Boston, MA: Pearson.

The National Counterintelligence Center (2011). Annual Report to Congress on Foreign Economic Collection and Industrial Espionage. Washington, DC: U.S. Government Printing Office.

Office of National Intelligence (2013). Retrieved from http://www.intelligence.gov/about-the-intelligence-community.

Richelson, J. T. (1999) *The US Intelligence Community*. Boulder, CO: Westview Press.

Heims, P. (1982). *Countering Industrial Espionage*. Surrey, UK: 20th Century Security Education.

Winker, I. (1997) *Corporate Espionage*. New York, NY: Prima Publishing.

3
CYBER ESPIONAGE

Cyber Industrial Espionage Defined

With the global use of the Internet, an entire new area for industrial espionage has been created. To protect your organization's assets, it is vital to understand the Internet and how it operates relative to networks and individual computers.

The Internet is an open global network supporting standard utilities such as e-mail, file transfer, news groups, and the World Wide Web. The World Wide Web is a set of graphical, hyper linked applications accessible over an organization's Internet. The Internet has opened a global communications medium and is used for internal communications, customer service and support, sales and distribution, electronic banking, marketing and research, and the storage of company confidential information as well as government classified information (Figure 3.1).

There are several types of websites. The interactive site can be customized for the user and is primarily utilized for one-to-one communications. The transaction site allows account inquiry and online transactions. Publishing websites provide reports, statistics, and other types of publications. Marketing websites offer online brochures or other sales vehicles.

Protection of the Internet and company and government information is the end-system user's responsibility. The threat to your system and information can come from hackers, competitors, governments, customers or clients, contractors or employees. They can cause havoc on the net through the destruction or modification of your data as will be discussed in this chapter.

While most states have laws relating to computer crime, it is also a federal offense and falls under *Title 18, Section 1030* and *Title 18, Section 2701* of the United States Code (U.S.C.). The FBI has primary jurisdiction over traditional investigations related to national defense,

Figure 3.1 Personal Computers must be considered with regard to Internet security. (Photo by Daniel J. Benny.)

foreign relations, or restricted data which can be used to cause damage to the United States. The US Secret Service has primary jurisdiction over criminal acts involving consumer reporting or US Treasury computers. The FBI and US Secret Service have concurrent jurisdiction over financial institutions fraud.

Cyber Espionage Indicators

Common Cyber Indicators

Any organization can be targeted for industrial espionage to include cyber espionage. The first step in preventing such threats is to have an understanding of the threat, the indicators of such threats and the counter espionage measures that can be deployed to stop or reduce the loss of protected information.

Common cyber indicators include:

- Phishing and spear phishing
- Malicious codes
- Weak and default passwords
- Unpatched or outdated software vulnerabilities
- Removal media

Phishing and Spear Phishing

Phishing is a high-tech scam that uses e-mail to deceive an individual into disclosing personal or company information. It puts one's personal information and the organization's information at a risk for cyber espionage.

Spear phishing is a variation of targeted phishing that is most often directed toward a specific individual or office within an organization. This might be done if there is specific information that the perpetrator seeks to obtain from a specific office or department in the organization or group of individuals.

Suspicious indicators that signal phishing and spear phishing include using e-mails written with bad grammar, misspellings, and/ or generic greetings. It may have maliciously-crafted attachments with varying file extensions or links to a malicious website. It may also appear to be sent from someone with a position of authority or a legitimate company such as a bank or credit card company, an online payment provider, or a federal, state or local government or law enforcement agency.

The e-mail may ask that the receiver update or validate information or click on a link. This may be reinforced with the threat of dire consequences or promises of a reward. The website that it directs one to will, in most cases, appear to be real, but of course it is not.

Spear phishing when utilized most often has a high level of targeting sophistication and appears to come from an associate, client, or acquaintance and may be relevant to the receiver's position in the company. It may even appear to be from the receiver's e-mail address book. The e-mail most often will contain graphics or logos that make the e-mail look legitimate.

The impact of a cyber espionage attack may result in the receiver disclosing protected or other useful information. This also allows the adversary to gain access to the receiver's and the organization's information and computer system.

Countermeasures include understanding and remaining alert to phishing and spear phishing. Never open and always delete suspicious e-mails. Do not click on suspicious links or attachments in e-mails. Do not call telephone numbers provided in suspicious e-mails and never disclose any information. Contact the company's security department and report any potential incidents and digital signatures. Ensure that anti-virus software and definitions are up to date and configure intrusion detection systems (IDS) to block malicious domains/IP address.

Malicious Code

Malicious code is software that damages and/or creates unwanted behaviors in the company's computer system. The malicious codes include viruses, Trojan horses, worms, key-loggers, spyware, rootkits, and backdoors. The cyber espionage attack can occur when e-mail attachments are opened, by the downloading of files, or by removable media.

The impact of such attacks includes corrupting files and destroying or modifying information, the compromise and loss of protected information, and allowing the hacker access to commit industrial espionage and then sabotaged company computer systems. Countermeasures that can be taken to guard against malicious code include viewing e-mail messages in plain text, using caution when opening e-mails, the scanning of all attachments, deleting e-mails from unknown senders, and turning off automatic downloading.

Methods of guarding against malicious codes in websites include blocking malicious links/IP addresses, blocking all unnecessary ports at the firewall and host, disabling unused protocols and services, and ensuring that the company operating system stays current with all operating system service packs and software security programs

Weak and Default Passwords

The use of weak and default passwords by employees of the company creates easily exploitable system vulnerabilities. Unacceptable passwords include those found in the dictionary including readily available information significant to the target person such as his or her name, date of birth or city where located. A lack of character diversity accounts for most hacked passwords. Passwords should have numbers and letters that both are upper and lower case and the same password should never be used on more than one application. Ineffective passwords can result in exploiting users' habit of repeating passwords across sites and systems, tracking passwords to less secure sites, and accessing the organization's protected information.

Countermeasures to prevent the hacking of passwords include combining letters, numbers, and special characters and never using personal information or common phrases or words. Do not write down passwords. Memorize them. Change passwords according to the organization's policy and there should be such a policy. Enforce account lockout for end-user accounts after a set number of retry attempts. Never save passwords or login credentials in the computer browser and, of course, do not share passwords.

Unpatched or Outdated Software Vulnerabilities

The use of unpatched or outdated software provides vulnerabilities and opportunities for adversaries to access information system. and cyber espionage. Signs of this type of activity include unauthorized system access attempts, unauthorized system access to or disclosure of information, unauthorized data storage or transmission, and unauthorized hardware and software modifications. All of these can lead to industrial espionage.

Indications of such attacks include but are not limited to corrupted or destroyed files, modified information, hard drive erasure and loss of information, hacker access, and sabotaged company computer systems.

To counter these threats, comply with the measures in the organization's policies, including the technology control plan (TCP), keep the system current with patches and updates, conduct frequent and unannounced computer audit—daily if possible and, if not, at least once each week. Do not rely on firewalls to protect against all attacks, they have their limits. Report intrusion attempts to IT security and the security department.

Removable Media

Removable media are all storage devices that can be added to and removed from a computer while the system is running. Adversaries seeking to take part in industrial espionage may use removable media to gain access to your system. Some of the examples of removable media include thumb drives, flash drives, DVDs, CDs and external hard drives.

Suspicious indicators related to removable media, espionage adversaries, and hackers may be the placing of removable media such as thumb drives at locations for personnel to pick up, or sending removable media to personnel under the guise of a prize or free product trial.

The effects could be quite damaging to the company and facilitate the espionage by allowing the hacker to steal information and also to sabotage systems on the way out efforts to reduce detection could result in in corrupt files and destroyed or modified company protected information.

Effective countermeasures to guard against removable media vulnerabilities include not using flash media unless operationally necessary, avoiding the use of any personally owned/non-company removable flash media on the company systems, and avoiding the use of company removable flash media on noncompany personal systems are essential because these could be infected. All data stored on removable media should be encrypted, if possible and affordable. This is a requirement when dealing with US government classified information. Encrypt in accordance with the data's classification or sensitivity level and use only removable media approved by your organization. If working with US government classified information, store in GSA approved storage containers at the appropriate level of classification.

Cyber Espionage Tradecraft

Those who take part in cyber espionage use tradecraft much like those taking part in traditional espionage. There are some differences working in the cyber world of espionage. The following are tradecraft methods attackers commonly use to launch cyber espionage attacks for the purpose of gaining access and retrieving protected company information.

Reconnaissance

As in all attempts at espionage, cyber spies will conduct research and identify the individuals they target through open source means. This may be either an individual whose computer they can access or someone they can turn into an asset.

Intrusion into the Network

Attackers send spear-phishing e-mails to targeted users within the company who have been identified by means of spoofed emails that include malicious links or attached malicious documents. The goal is to have one of the employees open the e-mail and click on the link, which then admits the attacker to commit industrial espionage.

Obtain User Credentials

If the cyber spy can obtain access to a company user's valid credentials or a domain administrator's credentials, the spy can retrieve much protected information.

Establish a Backdoor

If the domain administration credentials are obtained, the attackers can then move laterally within the company network, installing proverbial "backdoors" for future and continued exploitation and theft of protected information.

Install Multiple Utilities

This method includes the installation of utility programs on the company network to conduct system administration functions that can steal passwords, get e-mail, and list running processes.

Data Exfiltration

This is quite clever. The attacker obtains e-mails, attachments, and files from the company servers and then encrypts and exfiltrates the data via the attacker's command and control infrastructure.

Maintaining Persistence

For long-term cyber espionage, cyber spies must have continuous access to the company system. If the attackers suspect they are being detected or remediated, they will use other methods such as updating their malware to ensure that they don't lose their presence in the company network.

Use of Power Point as Cyber Espionage Tradecraft

I would like to thank my friend David Hook of Planehook Aviation Services LLC who provided the following information that he developed with his organization and granted permission to use it in this book

Insider Methods

- US Postal Service: sending an unauthorized letter with sensitive information enclosed
- Facsimile (FAX): transmitting an unauthorized fax with sensitive information included
- Attachments: sending an unauthorized email with sensitive information attached
- Verbal disclosure: conversations between an insider and an agent for a competitor or adversary

Counter Methods

- Mail operations: out-going mail screened for content, address, size and weight
- Fax operations: specific individuals authorized to send faxes, fax machine PINs

- Attachments: email systems and protocols established to limit use of attachment feature to specific individuals only
- Leak conversations: suspects are followed and observed

The use of the company Internet to hide information in a PowerPoint presentation is clever tradecraft that can be used for removal of protected company information. Illicit or compromised information and images can be hidden behind seeming legitimate images as a means of concealing proprietary information being taken through industrial espionage.

Internet-Based Social Networking Espionage

Internet-based social networking sites have created a revolution in social communication. Those taking part in industrial espionage use social networking to elicit information from employees of target companies.

These tactics are primarily used to exploit online social networks by espionage hackers who:

- Specialize in writing and manipulating computer code to gain access or install unwanted software on your computer or phone.
- Specialize in exploiting personal connections and manipulating people through social networks. They are also known as "social engineers."

If employees post information that may harm the company or information about themselves to a social networking site, that information is no longer private. The more information employees post, the more vulnerable they may become to espionage depending on what is disclosed about the company they work for or their own personal issues that can be used to manipulate or blackmail them. The personal information shared will be used to conduct attacks against the individual or company they work for. Espionage predators troll social networking sites looking for information or people to target for exploitation.

The ways Internet-based social networking can be used are exemplified in the following examples provided by the Federal Bureau of Investigation:

Before the 2010 World Cup, cybercriminals offered tickets for sale or sent phishing e-mails claiming recipients won tickets to see the event.

After the death of Osama Bin Laden, a video claiming to show Bin Laden's capture was posted on Facebook. The video was a fake. When users clicked on the link to the video, they were told to copy a JavaScript code into their browser bar which automatically sent the hoax to their friends, and gave the hackers full access to their account.

In March 2011, hackers sent two spear phishing emails to a small group of employees at security firm, RSA. They only needed one employee to open an infected file and launch the malware. The malware downloaded information from RSA that then helped the hackers learn how to defeat RSA's security token. In May and June 2011, a number of defense contractors' networks were breached via the compromised RSA token.

Advanced Persistent Threats

Advanced persistent threats (APTs) are cybercrimes directed at businesses, governments, and/or political targets. In most cases, APTs require a high degree of covert operations by a professional intelligence service over a prolonged duration in order to be successful. As a result, the attack continues beyond the immediate compromise of the system.

The most well-known recent case against private industry was the APT suffered by Google in 2010. This demonstrated that the target is not always government or military information. APTs can be used against any type of organization.

Those who take part in such activities are the foreign intelligence services, the highly-structured criminal operators, and/or terror organizations. Their goal is to utilize the full spectrum of computer intrusion technologies and techniques. While individual components of the attack may not be classed as particularly advanced, such organizations can access and develop more advanced tools as required to breach the systems by using combined multiple attack methodologies and tools in order to reach and compromise their target.

APTs are so damaging because they are persistent. The perpetrators give priority to a specific task, rather than opportunistically seeking immediate access to an organization's protected information. This implies that the attackers are guided by the desire to retrieve specific information. The attack is conducted through continuous monitoring and attempts to enter the protected system in order to obtain the desired information.

The threat from an APT is serious because the operation is conducted with a high level of coordination and the attackers are skilled, motivated, organized, and well funded.

Cyber Espionage Threats and Targets

Cyber espionage threats can come from many sources including the following:

- Insiders
- Hackers
- Cyber Criminals
- Terrorists
- Organized Crime
- Foreign Intelligence Entities

Insiders

Insiders are employees who take part in cyber espionage. Their motives and recruitment methods are the same as those employees who conduct the other types of espionage which were previously discussed. An insider may also be an agent who takes a position with the company as an employee or contractor in order to be inside the organization and thus gain access to the computer and protected information. The insider can cause the most damage and steal the greatest number of secrets. Additionally, this may be done over a long period of time.

Hackers

Hackers are those who attempt to gain access to the system. Their goal for the most part is to see if they can do it and then to cause damage to the computer system. Some will steal information just to pass it on in the World Wide Web or to sell for profit to anyone.

Cyber Criminals

These individuals most often are seeking access to information for which they can obtain money. This could include bank and credit card accounts.

Terrorists

Terror organizations attack computer systems for many reasons. Their efforts may be to disrupt the target, gain intelligence for an attack, or steal money or information to further their causes with funds and/or intelligence information.

Organized Crime

Criminal organization attacks on computers are usually for monetary gain. Fraud and money laundering are common tactics. They may also attempt access for intelligence information.

Foreign Intelligence Entities (Cyber Spies)

Other than insiders, foreign intelligence entities pose the most serious threats with regard to cyber espionage. They have professional and highly technical methods of breaching computer systems to steal information, control events, and damage or destroy the operating systems.

Cyber Espionage Targets

Sensitive company documents and proprietary information are always the target for cyber espionage and even more so if the company is a defense contractor dealing with US classified information. The target information is limitless. Examples include export controlled company and/or classified information and technology, information on DoD funded contracts, sensitive technological specification documents, users' login IDs and passwords, personal identification information

(SSN, date of birth, address) of company executives and employees, contact rosters and phone directories to be used to identify targets in the company. Other information that is sought includes technology information, which includes both classified and company unclassified, any militarily critical technology that would allow potential adversaries to make significant advances in the development, production, and use of military capabilities. Technology that has both military and commercial use is in high demand for theft.

Cyber Espionage Countermeasures

As in developing a traditional loss prevention program, you must conduct a risk assessment based on the projected use of the Internet and company computers and possible risk. Computer security procedures need to be based on neutralizing the greatest risk.

An effective computer security program designed to prevent industrial espionage has at least two levels of protection for the most sensitive information. It also treats the infrastructure and applications as two distinct but mutually dependent areas. In keeping with Astor's Fifth Law of Loss Prevention, "Any loss prevention control fails only upon audit." Ensure that there are strict monitoring and reporting procedures in place to support your security policy. Issues to consider are what services are allowed, what services or sites will be blocked, what usage is considered acceptable, how confidential are the e-mail and usage habits of employees, and how will the policy be enforced.

As part of your protection plan, minimize the number of connections to the Internet and control them. Increase the security of each connected computer and strengthen the network perimeter. The key factors in the protection of your assets through the Internet are the development of a sound security policy and the use of proxy firewalls when possible. Ensure that your firewall software is up to date and examine the security of modem connections to avoid end-runs. Conduct inspections and use penetration testing software against your system.

The threat is real and serious and countermeasures need to be put in place. Employees need to use complex alphanumeric passwords and change passwords regularly. They should not open an e-mail or attachment from an unfamiliar source, even if it looks official. They should not install or connect any personal software or hardware to their organization's network or hardware without permission from the IT department. Employees must be required to report all suspicious or unusual problems with their computers to the IT department

Management and IT departments need to implement defense in depth—a layered strategy that includes technical, organizational, and operational controls as well as technical defenses including firewalls, intrusion detection systems. Internet content filtering anti-virus software needs to be updated daily and vendor security patches should be regularly downloaded for all software. Ensure that required changes to the manufacturer's default passwords on all software are completed and that any attempted intrusions to your systems and networks should be monitored, logged, and analyzed.

Reportable suspicious cyber incidents, including the following, must be investigated at once:

- System failure or disruption
- Suspicious questioning
- Unauthorized access
- Unauthorized changes
- Suspicious e-mails
- Unauthorized use

By following these guidelines you can reduce the threat of loss through cyber espionage.

Cyber Espionage Awareness Training

The Defense Security Service offers an online cyber security course that covers the concepts of cyber espionage and various countermeasures. It can be taken by any organization and is of special value to those with classified government contracts. The course provides DoD personnel, contractors, and the government contracting agencies under the National Industrial Security Program Operating Manual (NISPOM) with an awareness of potential cyber threats directed against US technology and reporting requirements under the NISPOM and DoD Directive 5240.06.

The course introduces the automated information systems (AIS) environment and the threats and vulnerabilities faced when working within the government or defense industrial systems. It provides a working knowledge of cyber intrusion methods and cyber security countermeasures to assist employees in preventing cyber attacks and protecting their systems and information.

All company chief security officers are encouraged to use Defense Security Service sponsored training to provide cyber security awareness training for their personnel. Students completing this training will obtain training certificates.

Cyber Espionage Terms

Adware

This is software that displays an advertisement on the target computer by use of a popup. If clicked on, it may install itself on the computer, slowing the computer and may hijack the browser. The adware may also retrieve information from the computer or computer network and can be used for industrial espionage.

Anonymizing Proxies

This is the process is utilized when an employee or asset wants to hide his or her web browsing on a company computer. It also allows the user to bypass security filters that have been put in place.

AutoRun Worm

These malicious programs are able to access the computer through the Windows AutoRun feature on the target computer. They most often can invade the computer with the introduction of a USB device to spread the AutoRun worm.

Chain Letter or Email Malware

This email letter attempts to encourage the user to open the email and forward the email to other individuals. By clicking on the link, it allows a virus or Trojan into the computer. It may also be used to spread rumors and false information harmful to the organization or to send out e-mail under the company name.

Cookies

A cookie is a file that is inserted onto a computer to allow the website to remember information about the user. This, in itself, is not a security issue. The concern is that it can also be used to track the browsing history of the user for commercial marketing, and more importantly to obtain information for possible industrial espionage.

Data Theft, Leakage, or Loss

The unauthorized transfer of data and information from an organization's computer is called data theft, leak, or loss. This is one of the most common methods used for industrial espionage in passing on protected information on an organization's computer.

Denial of Service

This is an attack on an organization's computer network in order to prevent the authorized user from accessing websites and information on the company computer. Denial of service can be used to sabotage and disrupt the organization's computer system.

Domain Name System Hijacking

The attacker changes the domain name setting so that it is either ignored or controlled by another domain name. This provides the spy with access to the computer and information for industrial espionage.

Fraudulent Antivirus Malware

This alerts the computer user to a nonexistent virus in the computer so that the user will click on the link provided. This, in turn, allows the introduction of a real virus that can be used to obtain protected information.

Internet Worm

This is a virus that when opened will reproduce itself across the local computer network and even on the Internet. It may infect computers beyond those of the target company.

Keylogger

This is a device that is plugged into the computer that records all keystrokes. The keylogger is used by an individual wishing to take part in industrial espionage. The keylogger gives the asset the ability to identify the passwords on the computer. The asset will then be able to log into the computer at a later time using the stolen passwords undetected. Use of the password makes it appear that any information taken was taken by the person whose password was stolen.

Mobile Phone Malware

This malware is designed to run on a mobile and/or smart phone in order to retrieve all the information stored in the phone. This could include calls made and received, phone number, text messages, photographs, and applications accessed.

Phishing

Phishing is the process of sending out a fraudulent e-mail purporting to represent a legitimate organization such as a bank, or credit card company in attempt to induce the target to provided sensitive information. This will allow the perpetrator access to accounts, computers, and other sources of information.

Social Networking Threat

Using social networks creates a vulnerability to the threat of industrial espionage. This may result from providing too much open source information on sites such as Facebook. Information can also be obtained on social sites from the use of pretext attempts to illicit the information.

Spyware

Spyware, once installed on a computer, allows those taking part in espionage to retrieve information from the computer or computer network.

Trojan

The Trojan can be a serious threat because it can enter the computer by disguising itself as known software. Once downloaded, it adds itself to the computer start-up process. Spyware can monitor everything on the computer and even generate email.

Cyber Counterespionage Terms

Anti-Malware

This is software that can protect the information on the organization's computers from viruses, malware, worms, and Trojans. The anti-malware product scans the computer to identify unauthorized programs. Once the malware is identified, it can be destroyed thus eliminating the threat.

Anti-Spam

Anti-spam software can identify unwanted e-mail from reaching the inbox of the organization's computers. This is important because unwanted e-mails may be used to introduce viruses and malware into the system when opened. They can be used to obtain protected information. Not only does anti-spam software stop annoying e-mails, it also reduces the potential for industrial espionage.

Application Control

This is the process of blocking the use of identified applications that could compromise the security of the company's Internet system and information by the use of firewalls. This not only prevents the loss of information, but can be used to prevent staff from operating unauthorized applications in the company's Internet system.

Encryption

Encryption is the coding of information sent, received, and stored to prevent unauthorized access and theft of sensitive information. Encryption can only be read by individuals who are authorized and who are capable of decoding the encrypted information.

Firewall

A firewall is a barrier between computer networks to prevent malicious traffic that could be used to damage or retrieve information. In addition to preventing access, it can identify the threat and provide a warning that an attempt was made and has been blocked.

Intrusion Prevention System

This is a system that monitors all activity on a company's computers and provides notification of threats or problems that it identifies. It is not only a preventive tool, but also an investigative aid in identifying the operative who launched the attack.

Network Access Control

This includes the authorization of those employees who are authorized to enter the system. It also includes the assessment of those trying to enter the system and the enforcement of company security policies.

URL Content Filtering

This software blocks categories or specific websites that the organization does not want staff accessing from company computers. This not only prevents staff from browsing nonwork related websites, but also protects against viruses that may be introduced into the system when unauthorized websites are opened.

Bibliography

Association of Certified Fraud Examiners (2000). *Corporate Espionage*. Austin, TX: Association of Certified Fraud Examiners.

Central Intelligence Agency (2012) *Factbook*. Washington, DC: U.S. Government Printing Office.

Defense Security Service (2013) Retrieved from http://www.dss.mil/

Heims, P. (1982). *Countering Industrial Espionage*. Surrey, UK: 20th Century Security Education.

David Hook (2012) Planehook Aviation Services LLC.

Johnson, W.M. (2007). *Business Espionage*. Shoreline, WA: Questor Group.

Martin, S. (2005) *Business Intelligence and Corporate Espionage*. Boston, MA: Pearson.

The National Counterintelligence Center (2011). Annual Report to Congress on Foreign Economic Collection and Industrial Espionage. Washington, DC: U.S. Government Printing Office.

Office of National Intelligence (2013). Retrieved from http://www.intelligence.gov/about-the-intelligence-community

Richelson, J. T. (1999) *The US Intelligence Community*. Boulder, CO: Westview Press.

Heims, P. (1982). *Countering Industrial Espionage*. Surrey, UK: 20th Century Security Education.

Winker, I. (1997) *Corporate Espionage*. New York, NY: Prima Publishing.

4

Developing a Counterespionage Program

Conducting a Counterespionage Risk Assessment

Before an effective counterespionage program can be developed there must be a risk assessment of the facility and information to be protected to identify the risk of espionage against the protected information of the organization. When determining the risk, one needs to examine the information to be protected, the value of such information, define who would want it, determine how accessible it is, and the impact on the organization should such information be illegally obtained through industrial espionage. Once the threat and risk have been identified, one needs to establish what must be protected. Next, determine the severity of the threat and probability of occurrence.

Threat: (risk of threat = severity of threat × probability of occurrence).

This is accomplished by making an examination to determine the required security to prevent or reduce the threats. The next step is to identify the measures to be implemented in order to reduce the threat.

An inventory of the protected information needs to be conducted by looking at all hard copies and computer-based information. The value of the information to the organization needs to be assessed from both a financial and criticality of operations perspective. Based on the type of information and mission of the organization there needs to be an assessment as to who would want such information and how it could be utilized if obtained through industrial espionage.

Additional areas for examination in the risk assessment process include reviewing how the information—hard copies, and computer-based data—are currently being protected. This will begin with a review of physical security working from the perimeter of the facility inward to where the information is stored, be it in a security container or computer. The risk assessment should also review security force operations, computer security, and personnel security issues in the human resources department.

This risk assessment also needs to examine the counterespionage awareness training program currently in place for employees of the facility including the information provided in the training sessions, hand-outs provided to participants, and documentation of such training in employee personnel files.

Details on what specifically to examine when conducting the risk assessment as it relates to physical security, security force operation, computer security, human resources operations and awareness training is provided in Chapter 8.

As part of the risk assessment process, it is important to remember the five requirements for someone to take part in espionage:

- Motive
- Opportunity
- Rationalization
- Ability
- Trigger

When developing the counterespionage plan the goal is to remove one or more of these five requirements in order to thwart industrial espionage. There are four primary reasons that an individual taking part in espionage is discovered:

- Reported by a source in an intelligence service
- Turned in by an acquaintance or family member
- The perpetrator's own mistake
- Effective counterespionage plan and program

As one can see, a primary reason for the detection of a spy is the counterespionage plan and program established by the organization.

The Counterespionage Plan

Once a risk assessment has been completed, the results will be utilized to develop the counterespionage plan. This plan needs to encompass all protective measures that will be utilized including all areas identified in the risk assessment as well as physical security measures and procedures, security force operational procedures, and computer security measures. Human recourse procedures related to recruitment, background investigations, and termination procedures also need to be covered in the plan. The types and methods of security awareness training must also be included in the plan as well as employee training documentation.

Methods of internal audits to prevent industrial espionage and the frequency of such audits should be in the counterespionage plan. The criteria for conducting counterespionage investigations must also be identified. Additional considerations will include which events will trigger such an investigation and along with pinpointing who will be responsible for conducting the investigation.

The counterespionage plan needs to be in writing. Furthermore, it should be written in an easy-to-read format and disseminated to all employees who need to know its contents. A three-hole punch format is recommended. By utilizing this format, updates can easily be made because outdated pages can be discarded and new information inserted. This eliminates the need for publishing the entire plan every time the plan is updated.

The counterespionage plan must be updated as policies and procedures change. At a minimum, the counterespionage plan needs to be examined and updated at least once a year. If there are no updates or changes, the document should be reviewed to establish that it is current.

Never place any procedure or policy in the plan that cannot be accomplished. Should legal action arise related to the counterespionage program, that procedure or policy can be obtained through subpoenas and other forms of legal discovery. If an organization states in its counterespionage plan that the organization has a specific policy and that policy is not being followed, the organization's own counterespionage plan can be used against it in court for failure to follow its own standards and procedures.

Counterespionage Awareness Training

It is important to provide all employees with counterespionage awareness training as a proactive measure in the prevention of espionage. If employees understand the threat and the methods of collection, they will be able to recognize possible espionage or attempts to have information obtained from them. The employees must also be instructed on how and to whom they report such a threat.

In the National Counterintelligence Center's 2011 Annual Report to Congress on Foreign Economic Collection and Industrial Espionage, an overview of what should be included in counterespionage awareness training was provided. That information is provided below as an excellent example of what should be considered in presenting the counterespionage awareness training.

THE INTELLIGENCE THREAT

The gathering of information by intelligence agents is a strategy for gaining superiority over enemies. Intelligence officers are those individuals working for government intelligence services who are trained to serve their country by gathering information. Spies betray their countries and or their employers by committing espionage. There is an increase in a different kind of spying as espionage is based on not only the theft of classified information but also on theft of high-technology information, classified or unclassified.

Industrial espionage is the acquisition by foreign governments or individuals of US high-technology information in order to enhance their countries, organizations, or clients. According to the National Counterintelligence Center, the FBI believes that nearly one hundred countries are now running economic espionage operations against the United States. Targets are shifting away from the classified military information sought in the days of the Cold War toward basic research and development processes in which private organizations take part. Targets also include technology and trade secrets including everything from cost analyses, marketing plans, contract bids, and proprietary software to the high-tech data itself. Often the technology is not a physical product; it may be a plan, formula or an idea that can be transported on computer or fax machine, or simply carried away inside the minds of scientists.

METHODS OF ESPIONAGE

Industrial espionage is frequently conducted by using fundamental business intelligence-gathering methods. The Internet and dozens of commercial databases are generally available, along with sources such as trade journals, company newsletters, and annual reports. Employees need to be alert to activities such as extracting information from executives of competing companies under the guise of job interviews, or hiring away an employee from a competitor just to acquire that person's knowledge.

A major means those in espionage from other countries use to obtain information is to send their representatives to the United States on fact-finding visits or for training. Participants in scientific meetings, trade delegations, and trade shows can easily obtain useful information during their stays here. Other arrangements, such as visitor programs, cultural exchanges and military exchanges, are also used. One method is to send students and scholars to universities or government research laboratories where they are trained and also participate in research as guests of the government. High-tech data, acquired by scientists participating in such programs, is easily transferred back to their home countries through fax, telephone, the written word, and memory.

Often foreigners acquire proprietary information under the guise of market research, sending surveys from abroad to ferret out product information. Even personal telephone calls, letters, and fax inquiries from abroad can elicit useful information. Callers may pretend to be someone other than who they are; in the parlance of the business intelligence fraternity, this is known as pretext calling. Some industrial espionage cases resemble typical old-style espionage operations conducted with the full panoply of tradecraft. Indeed, the very words used to describe the roles of participants in an economic espionage crime are borrowed directly from the classic espionage lexicon: spies, moles, recruiters, and defectors.

The most effective method is to acquire information from an organization or company in classic spy style by recruiting a mole on the inside or by sending an operative who poses as someone else. Another method is to blackmail vulnerable employees of companies or to recruit foreign nationals working in US subsidiaries abroad. Not all spies have been recruited. Some perhaps disgruntled or troubled employees, past or present, of US companies have stolen materials and then sold them to foreign companies—the classic espionage volunteer.

Equally as unscrupulous, and also patently illegal, is the outright bribing of employees to steal plans, reports, and other proprietary documents, or hiring consultants to spy on competitors, a practice that can include bugging competitors' offices. Other methods include theft and smuggling of goods, theft of intellectual property, tampering with companies' electronics, and bribery.

INDICATORS OF INDUSTRIAL ESPIONAGE

Studies of industrial espionage cases have revealed a pattern of warning signs displayed by several spies in varying degrees. The most common indicators of an individual's espionage activity or potential vulnerability to espionage are mentioned below and should be a matter of concern to security and supervisory personnel.

Signs that an individual might be involved in espionage include attempts to gain access to classified information without a valid need-to-know or without the required security clearance.

Other indicators include unauthorized reproduction or removal of classified material from the work area and secret destruction of documents. Unexplained affluence can be a possible sign of ongoing espionage if a legitimate source of increase income cannot be found. Sudden prosperity might be of particular concern when it follows a period of financial difficulty.

Foreign travel, on a regular basis and without sufficient explanation, may also be another sign of espionage when individuals with access to classified information are involved. Job and career dissatisfaction or deep grudges against the company or the United States government have also figured as predisposing elements in some cases.

Industrial espionage against the United States and private organizations continues to occur, and the threat it poses to national security and economic well-being of a private organization is immense. The current challenge for security professionals is to make employees understand that, despite the vast political changes around the globe, foreign intelligence activities really do continue to be directed against the United States. Many people believe that there is no longer the danger of espionage. The threat is real and ongoing.

Benjamin Pierce Bishop, a 59-year old employee of an unnamed defense contractor, was arrested in December 2012 and accused of possessing and passing on national military secrets including nuclear weapons information to a foreign national. Bishop was a former U.S. Army officer and was working at US Pacific Command in Oahu, Hawaii. He had been romantically involved with a 27-year old Chinese woman whom he met at an international military defense conference. Several classified documents were found in his home and he had allegedly been passing secret information to her for a period of nineteen months from May 2011 through December 2012. Bishop has had top secret security clearance since July of 2002. The information turned over allegedly included data concerning US nuclear weapons and the deployment of such weapons and systems as well as the early warning radar systems and the United States' ability to detect ballistic missiles. He faces up to twenty years in jail if convicted.

Counterespionage When Traveling

When traveling for business especially in foreign countries, there is always the threat of being targeted for industrial espionage. In many countries upon entering or when checking into a hotel, the traveler's passport may be photocopied and detailed information is requested. This is because in many countries the state security service stops by hotels each day and examines the passports and information provided by the traveler. Depending on the traveler's identity and occupation, that person may be targeted for espionage.

The key to understanding counterespionage—especially when traveling in foreign countries such as China and Russia—is to assume that the traveler is under continued surveillance. All conversations on the phone and in rooms are monitored and recorded. It is also important to be aware that all e-mails sent or received are intercepted and monitored. Assume that all luggage may be searched covertly at the hotel or in transit.

Be alert to contacts with individuals who probe for information on occupation, company details, and personal information. Travelers should not place themselves in a situation where they may be compromised and blackmailed.

Situational awareness is vital. Be alert to the surroundings and all that is taking place. Trust no one. This situational awareness can be viewed as a color coded method:

- White: Unaware of one's own surrounding. Easy to become a victim.
- Green: Alert and aware using all senses, sight, hearing, smell, taste, and touch. One can operate in this mode continuously.
- Yellow: Become aware of potential threat and evaluate.
- Red: Immediate action is required to repel the threat.

By following this simple color coded model for situational awareness, the threat of espionage can be prevented or reduced.

The following guidelines are suggested when traveling in country or abroad in the prevention of industrial espionage.

Travel Preparations

Travel Itinerary

- Leave a complete itinerary with your office and with family to included contact numbers if known.

Passport

- Make sure your passport will be valid for the duration of the trip.
- Make three copies of the passport page containing your photography. Place one in your carry-on bag, one in your checked baggage, and leave one with your family.

Visas

- Make sure that you have the appropriate visa and that it is current.
- Visa application information must be accurate. False information may be grounds for incarceration.

Documents

- Take only the credit cards you will need.
- Carry in your wallet or purse only the documents you will need.
- Realize that any document you carry may be subject to search, seizure, or copying.
- Carry a US driver's license with a photo on it.
- Make two copies of the numbers of your credit cards and traveler's checks, airline tickets, and the telephone numbers to report a loss.

Luggage

- Use a covered luggage tag to place your name on the outside of the luggage.
- Put your name and address on the inside of your luggage.
- Use sturdy luggage and do not over-pack.
- Never leave your luggage unattended as it could be stolen or used by terrorists.
- Do not transport items for others. Any gifts received from a foreign contact should be thoroughly inspected before being placed in your luggage.
- When at the hotel and when returning home, inspect your luggage for any monitoring devices that many have been concealed in the luggage.

Transportation Hub Security

To diminish the risk of becoming a victim of attempted espionage, remember the following:

- Check in early then go directly to the security checkpoint and into the secure area.
- Ensure that you have visual contact with all luggage as you pass the security check point so that it is not stolen.
- Always be aware of your surroundings.
- Arrange to be met upon arrival if possible. Preplan transportation to and from the airport.

Hotel Security

Planning

- Use hotels recommended by your travel agent where possible.
- Make your own reservation and ensure that the room is guaranteed.
- Request information about hotel parking, security, and fire safety.

Arriving at and Departing from Hotel

- Disembark as close to the hotel entrance as possible and in a lighted area. Before exiting the vehicle, ensure there are no suspicious persons and activities in the area.
- Do not linger or wander around the parking lot or indoor garage.
- Watch for distractions that may be staged for an espionage contact.
- Hand-carry valuable papers and items to your room; do not give them to a bellman.

Check-in

- Keep control of your luggage during registration to prevent access and avoid the concealment of surveillance devices.
- In some countries, your passport may be held by the hotel for review by the police or other authorities. If so, retrieve it at the earliest possible time.
- Review room security such as the key and access control, auxiliary lock, window locks, and safes.
- Note how the hotel staff dresses, the types of uniforms and the identification badges. Verify hotel employees with the front desk before permitting entry into your room.

Counterespionage Security in a Foreign Country

- Assume that all locations including hotel rooms are monitored.
- Keep your hotel room key with you at all times.
- Keep your hotel room door locked at all times.
- At night, utilize a portable door alarm and secure your passport and other valuables.
- Invest in a good map of the city. Note the location of your hotel, police, US Embassy and hospital.
- Have situational awareness at all times and try to blend in.
- Do not carry your passport or money in pockets accessible to pick pockets.
- Keep your passport with you at all times.

- Vary the times you leave and return to the hotel and avoid patterns.
- Avoid persons you do not know.

Personal Conduct

- Do not do anything that might be misconstrued, reflect poorly on your personal judgment, or be embarrassing to you or your company and could be used for blackmail.
- Do not carry, use, or purchase any narcotics, marijuana, or other abused drugs. Many countries have very stringent laws related to drugs.
- Do not let a friendly ambiance and alcohol override your good sense and capacity when it comes to social drinking.
- Do not engage in black market activities.
- Do not carry any political or religious tracts or brochures likely to be offensive in the host country.
- Do not carry pornography or radical publications.
- Do not photograph anything that appears to be associated with military, internal security or restricted areas.

Arrested! What Do I Do Now?

Foreign police and intelligence agencies detain persons for myriad reasons including suspicion, curiosity, or intelligence reasons. The best advice is to exercise good judgment, be professional in your demeanor.

- Ask to contact the US embassy or consulate. As a citizen of another country, you have this right, but that does not mean the host country will allow you to do so right away. Continue to make the request.
- Stay calm, maintain your dignity, and do not provoke the arresting officer(s).
- Admit nothing and volunteer nothing.
- Sign nothing.
- Accept no one at face value. Ask for identification. TRUST NO ONE.

Counterespionage Audits

Audits are a critical part of any counterespionage program. The goal of the audits is to determine if all of the policies, procedures and physical security measures related to the safeguarding of protected and classified information are being adhered to. As 1960's loss prevention consultant Sal Astor stated in his Astor's Laws of Loss Prevention, a loss prevention program will only fail upon audit. In other words, if an organization conducts no audits on its counterespionage program, the organization will not know that there is a problem or a failure in the system until a loss occurs and such loss is discovered. With no audits, there is the assumption that all is fine, but that is, of course, a false sense of security. After protected information has been compromised is not the time that an organization should be become aware of such a loss.

All areas related to the counterespionage program should be audited on a regular basis and surprise audits should be conducted as well. This would include audits of the protected information in which the inventory is examined to ensure that all information is accounted for. The audit should also include an inspection of the documents and information to ensure that they are properly marked, kept in security storage, and that access to security containers or computer systems that contain documents and protected information is restricted and documented.

The list of cleared company employees who have access must also be reviewed during each audit to ensure that those individuals are still authorized and have access only to information on a need-to-know basis. Documentation of cleared employee security awareness training should also be verified during the audit process.

Computer system passwords and security container combinations must be memorized and not written down. During audits, attention needs to be given to computer passwords or security container combinations that may have been written down in areas where they could be located by an individual intent on committing industrial espionage.

Counterespionage Investigations

Counterespionage investigations are conducted to determine whether or not industrial espionage or other intelligence activities such as planning for sabotage, assassination, or terrorist actions by or on behalf of a foreign government, criminal organization, company, person or terrorists group are present.

When conducting the counterespionage investigation, the concepts of inductive and deductive reasoning should be applied. Inductive reasoning is the process of observing a set of characteristics based on a premise of broad generalizations and statistical analysis which leads to the development of a hypothesis. Deductive reasoning is the process of observing a set of characteristics that may be reasoned from a convergence of physical and a behavioral actions or patterns within an event or a series of events such as a crime or serious of crimes.

The theories of inductive and deductive reasoning have been valuable tools in the investigation profession for more than one hundred and twenty years. These theories have been utilized in the investigation of traditional criminal offenses such as robberies, thefts, fraud, and burglaries. They have also been extensively used in the investigation of criminal profiling of serial killers, sexual predators, drug dealers, organized crime, and, as seen since September 11, 2001, in uncovering suspected members of international and national terrorist organizations. This is an excellent approach to the investigation of industrial espionage.

The most recognized and famous use of the concepts of inductive and deductive reasoning is in the works of Sir Arthur Conan Doyle in the Sherlock Holmes canon of novels and short stories, which first appeared in 1892. Doyle's fictional detective Sherlock Holmes utilized these theories not only to solve crimes, but to build profiles of individuals based on observations of the facts and then building a hypothesis around the facts. Holmes also used this method in the investigation of espionage such as the Naval Treaty and the Bruce-Partington Plan.

Inductive Reasoning

Inductive reasoning is the use of an inference that has been established through a set of observations leading to a generalization, which is known as a premise. The premise is a working assumption. While a working assumption has been established, it does not mean automatically that it is a valid assumption.

The inductive argument or assumption investigates issues in the case from the specific to the general and is known as inductive generalization. A conclusion would be formed about observations and characteristics of a single individual or single event. It may also include the characteristics and observations of several individuals or events. Based on that information, a preliminary generalization is made concluding that similar individuals or events that are seen or encountered in the future will exhibit the same observations of the originally documented characteristics.

Deductive Reasoning

Deductive reasoning involves the argument that if the premise is true, then the conclusion is also true. Within deductive reasoning, the conclusions are reached through the given premises. The reasoning moves from the general to the specific when utilized in a criminal investigation for espionage. Applied to the offender's behaviors and/or patterns the reasoning would be suggestive of critical offender characteristics.

Deductive reasoning includes looking at a set of the offender's characteristics that are reasoned by the convergence of all of the physical evidence in the case as well as the behavioral evidence patterns within that case or a serious of related espionage cases and crimes.

Counterespionage investigations should be conducted at any point in time when there is a violation of security policy. Such an investigation may also be based on a report of adverse information or indications of industrial espionage are taking place.

Security violations may be identified during the counterespionage audit or they may be reported to security. All violations need to be adequately investigated in order to identify the violation and determine who was involved. The investigation should be used to correct the situation and remove the risk of industrial espionage. Some of the most common violations include:

- Classified material left out or unattended
- Unsecured, unattended security containers/unsecured combinations
- Removal of material without approval
- Loss of classified information

- Unauthorized copying or destruction of classified material
- Unauthorized/improper transmission of classified material
- Disclosure of/permitting access by an unauthorized person
- Processing classified material on a nonapproved computer
- Passwords left in view
- Combinations to security containers left in view

If the organization is operating under the rules and policies of the National Industrial Security Program Operating Manual (NISPOM), cleared defense contractor employees are required to report adverse information regarding other cleared employees to their respective security departments. This includes adverse information that reflects unfavorably on the trustworthiness or reliability of these employees and suggests that their ability to safeguard classified information may be impaired.

This adverse information may include excessive indebtedness and financial problems, unexplained affluence, use of drugs or excessive use of intoxicants, unusual behaviors, mental or emotional problems, and criminal activity and convictions. Adverse information should be reported to protect the individual from being placed in a position where he or she could be exploited and persuaded to commit a security violation, or even espionage. Many espionage cases can be cited in which a human weakness was exploited by hostile intelligence agents.

Most often the espionage investigation will begin with the detection of the offense of espionage. It may be determined that information is missing, it has been leaked to the press, or that a competitor is using the company's protected information. It is vital to determine how the information was compromised to prevent it in the future. If one finds the method of compromise, it is likely that the perpetrator will also be identified.

The means of compromise is varied. It could in fact be accidental. This could occur as the result of an overheard conservation, or mistakenly released in an e-mail or web site. The information might have been obtained by means of deception or a pretext involving an innocent employee. Inadequate protocols or failure to follow security procedures may be a reason such as a document left about or not shredded in the proper manner. There is also, of course, the possibility of human or technical surveillance and the recruitment of an employee as a spy.

Technical penetration could also have come by means of the computer system. While not the most likely means, information could have been removed by a covert physical penetration of the facility.

If accidental and procedure failures are ruled out, the next step is to focus on the individual or individuals closest to the protected information that was compromised. Once the individuals have been identified, a current covert background investigation needs to be conducted. This background investigation should determine if those identified show recent risk factors. These factors include financial or lifestyle changes that appear out of the ordinary. Signs to look for include spending money that does not match the individual's income, financial hardship, addiction or other issues that might result in possible

If the individuals closest to the information are cleared, the circle needs to be expanded to other employees and contractors. Visitor logs should be examined and interviews conducted. A review of all security measures should also be conducted along with an examination of security camera recordings, access control data logs, phone calls and email records.

The investigation may further lead to conducting a technical surveillance counter measures (TSCMs) sweep to determine technical surveillance was used to compromise the information that was taken.

Counterespionage Technical Surveillance Counter Measures (TSCMs)

Technical surveillance counter measures refers to the process of detecting, identifying and remove eavesdropping devices that are recording or transmitting conversations or sending real-time video to unauthorized individuals for the purpose of industrial espionage. The use of technical surveillance counter measures needs to be considered a part of every counterespionage program.

The detection of such devices is not as simple as it used to be. It is no longer a matter of simply looking behind photos and under lamps to locate listening devices. With today's new technology, such surveillance devices are miniature and easily concealed in everyday objects. Detecting such devices requires the use of complex technical surveillance counter measures technical services and equipment. An organization can buy such equipment for its security department and have an individual trained in the operation of the technical surveillance counter measures equipment. That individual can then be designated as the technical surveillance counter measures expert for the organization and conduct regular technical surveillance counter measures sweeps of the facility. The cost of such equipment will vary. For example, Research Electronics International, one of the most prestigious suppliers of technical surveillance counter measures equipment, can provide the CPM-700 Deluxe Countermeasure package for around $4,000. This package can detect and locate sophisticated eavesdropping transmitters both digital and analog including RF audio, video, and data units. It will also detect infrared and carrier current transmitters. The package allows for the testing of telephone and miscellaneous wiring for monitoring devices. Research Electronics International also provides classroom and practical exercises on all of the technical surveillance counter measures that they sell.

The other option is to contract such service with a professional technical surveillance counter measures firm. These experts are very knowledgeable about the profession and have extensive training in the operation of the detection equipment and experience in electronics, radio transmitters, receivers, telephone and computer systems, and video transmission as methods of surveillance for the purpose of industrial espionage. The one time cost for a contracted technical surveillance counter measures sweep can range between $2,000 to $5,000 depending on the perceived or known threat and the area to be swept for monitoring devices. Sweeps can be conducted anywhere from a few hours to several days depending on the number of rooms and the area that needs to be swept and protected.

By utilizing technical surveillance counter measures as part of an organization's counterespionage program, whether a propriety technical surveillance counter measures expert or a contractor, it is vital to the protection of protected company information. It will help protect the privacy of the organization by reducing the risk of unauthorized monitoring.

Technical surveillance counter measures sweeps should be done on a regular basis but based on a random schedule. Surprise sweeps should also be conducted. These surprise sweeps are very effective in thwarting eavesdroppers in that they cannot remove their equipment as they can before a regularly scheduled bug sweep. Areas in the organization that should receive scheduled technical surveillance counter measures sweeps include the following:

- Executive offices
- Executive residences
- Corporate apartments
- Vehicles (cars, aircraft, boats)
- Executive mobile phones
- Home phones (landlines)
- Board rooms
- Off-site business meeting rooms
- Security office

Depending on the size of the facility, other areas may also be included in a scheduled sweep. If there is an indication of a threat from unauthorized monitoring, a technical surveillance counter measures sweep should be done at once. Indicators that information is being compromised through such monitoring may include:

- Lose of a bid or request for proposal that you would normally win
- Unexplained decrease in new sales
- Company business strategies are revealed
- Pricing and sales strategy is known by your competitors
- Contract negotiations for labor and contracts are increasingly more difficult
- Company protected information and trade secrets are exposed
- Confidential employee information is released
- Company financial information is released

Bibliography

Association of Certified Fraud Examiners (2000). *Corporate Espionage*. Austin, TX: Association of Certified Fraud Examiners.
Central Intelligence Agency (2012). *Factbook*. Washington, DC: U.S. Government Printing Office.
Defense Security Service (2013). Retrieved from http://www.dss.mil/
Douglas, J. (1995). *Mind Hunter*. New York, NY: Simon & Schuster Inc.
Heims, P. (1982). *Countering Industrial Espionage*. Surrey, UK: 20th Century Security Education.
Johnson, W.M. (2007). *Business Espionage*. Shoreline, WA: Questor Group.

Martin, S. (2005). *Business Intelligence and Corporate Espionage*. Boston, MA: Pearson.

The National Counterintelligence Center (2011). Annual Report to Congress on Foreign Economic Collection and Industrial Espionage. Washington, DC: U.S. Government Printing Office.

Office of National Intelligence (2013). Retrieved from http://www.intelligence.gov/about-the-intelligence-community

Research Electronic International. (2013). Retrieved form http://www.research-electronics.com/cgi-bin/main.cgi

Richelson, J. T. (1999). *The US Intelligence Community*. Boulder, CO: Westview Press

Turvey, B. (2001). *Criminal Profiling*. San Diego, CA: Elsevier Academic Press.

Heims, P. (1982). *Countering Industrial Espionage*. Surrey, UK: 20th Century Security Education.

Winker, I. (1997). *Corporate Espionage*. New York, NY: Prima Publishing.

5

PROTECTING PROPRIETARY AND US GOVERNMENT CLASSIFIED INFORMATION

Identifying Information to be Protected

In order to protect the vital information within an organization, it must first be identified. When dealing with nongovernment classified information where there are designated levels of classification, a private organization can develop any level of classification it desires. The classification designation of a protected company should not be given the same classification name as government classified information: confidential, secret and top secret. If those designations were used it would confuse the company information with government information. Examples of company classifications may include:

Company restricted
Company confidential
Company classified
Company protected

Marking of Protected Information

Each protected document should have a color coded cover sheet with the highest level of classification as provided in the examples given. Each page of the protected document should have the company classification at both the top and bottom of the page.

For other media such as computer disks, flash drives, DVDs, videos, cinematic films or photographs, the highest level of information on the media should be placed on the front of the media. Non-paper media should be marked by the use of self-adhesive stickers marked and color coded to the company information classification system.

Secure Storage of Protected Information

When securing company protected information, it is vital to have the documents or media stored in security containers or safes. These security containers should be high quality commercial products such as a Liberty safe (See Figure 5.1).

Figure 5.1   Liberty safe. (Photo by Dr. Daniel J. Benny)

To ensure the protection of company sensitive information, the security containers and safes should meet the requirements of US General Services Administration approved security containers Classes 1 to 3. All security containers approved by GSA bear a GSA Approved Security Container label affixed to the front of the security container. They are classified as follows:

Class 1

The security container is insulated for fire protection. And the protection provided is:

30 man-minutes against surreptitious entry
10 man-minutes against forced entry
1 hour protection against fire damage to content
20 man-hours against manipulation of the lock
20 man-hours against radiological attack

Class 2

The security container is insulated for fire protection and the protection provided is:

20 man-minutes against surreptitious entry
1 hour protection against fire damage to contents
5 man-minutes against forced entry
20 man-hours against manipulation of the lock
20 man-hours against radiological attack

Class 3

The security container is not insulated and the protection provided is:

20 man-minutes against surreptitious entry
20 man-hours against manipulation of the lock
20 man-hours against radiological attack
No forced entry requirement

Security Filing Cabinets

Security filing cabinets are available in a variety of styles to include single, two, four, and five drawers and in both letter size and legal size models.

Secure Destruction of Protected Information

Methods of Destruction

There are numerous methods for destroying company protected information when it is no longer needed. This information may be on paper or some other medium. It is important to completely destroy protected information when no longer needed so it cannot be retrieved by unauthorized individuals.

Paper Records   The most effective method is to shred the documents. Cross shredding is recommended to insure that the documents are completely destroyed. At no time, should protected documents be recycled. Burning of the protected paper records ensures complete destruction. Documents need to be burned in accordance with any environmental guidelines and local burning restrictions. An approved incinerator must also be utilized.

Electronic Media   Erasing or deleting information or even reformatting the hard drive does not prevent the information from being recovered. All that is removed are the logical pointers to the information. Sanitization is the process by which data is removed from information technology equipment and storage media and rendered unrecoverable. In general, those involved in industrial espionage cannot retrieve data that has been sanitized. There are two acceptable methods that may be used for the removal of records from electronic media:

- Overwriting
- Physical destruction

Overwriting is a method of clearing data from media (hard drives, rewritable disks, etc.) that will be reused. Low-level overwriting or clearing of data is a process of deleting files using a specialized program that removes information from storage media in a manner that renders it unreadable, unless special utility software or techniques are used to recover the cleared data. It also erases all partition tables and drive formats. There are many products with varying price structures available. However, the product selected must support any size hard drive; permanently erase operating systems, program files, and data. In other words, it must be capable of erasing all data from the physical hard drive.

Low-level overwriting is a process that is best used for the removal of data from computers that will continue to be used. High-level overwriting or reformatting of data is the replacing of previously stored data on a drive or disk with a predetermined pattern of meaningless information. This effectively renders the data unrecoverable. Software products and applications used for the overwriting process should meet these specifications: sanitization is not complete until three overwrite passes and a verification passage have been completed; the software should have the capability to overwrite the entire hard disk drive, making it impossible to recover any meaningful data; the software must have the capability to overwrite using a minimum of three cycles of data patterns on all sectors, blocks, tracks, and any unused disk space on the entire hard disk medium; the software must have a method to verify that all data has been removed; sectors not overwritten must be identified.

Physical Destruction   If the operable hard drive is to be removed from service completely, it should be physically destroyed or sanitized. If the hard drive is inoperable or has reached the end of its useful life, it should be physically destroyed. Hard drives should be destroyed when they are defective or cannot be repaired or sanitized for reuse. Physical destruction must be accomplished to an extent that precludes any possible further use of the media. This can be attained by removing the hard drive from the cabinet and removing any steel shielding materials and/or mounting brackets and cutting the electrical connection to the hard drive unit. The hard drive should then be subjected to enough physical force or extreme temperatures that will disfigure, bend, mangle, or otherwise mutilate the hard drive so it cannot be reinserted into a functioning computer.

Removable Media   Due to the relatively low cost of removable storage media, the best advice for all media that cannot be reused is to physically destroy the media.

Magnetic media (tape, floppy disk) are records stored on magnetic media can be reformatted. Reformatting is the process of deleting files using a specialized program that removes information from the media in a manner that renders it unreadable, unless special utility software or techniques are used to recover the cleared data.

Nonelectronic and Nonpaper Media   DVDs, videos, cinematographic films and microforms (microfilm/fiche/aperture cards/x-rays) can be destroyed by shredding, cutting, crushing or chemical recycling.

Protection of US Classified Information

Much of the classified information that falls under the US government's classified information program is generated by contractors. These contactors include universities and private industry. Much of the industrial espionage from private industry and universities includes attempts to obtain information of value to industry but also information that is covered under the US government classified information program. When developing a counterespionage program, a review of this classification system must be included for those contractors conducting such research, development, and production for the US government.

The protection of government classified information is vital. Two 2008 espionage investigations are examples for the need of protecting classified information. A Defense Department analyst and a former engineer for Boeing Company were accused in separate spy cases with helping to deliver military secrets to the Chinese government. In addition, two immigrants, one from China and one from Taiwan, were accused of working with the defense analyst. This fact was determined after an FBI raid of the immigrant's home in New Orleans where one of them lived resulted in their arrest.

These arrests demonstrate China's recent attempts to gain top secret information about US military systems and sales. This is an example of how adept China is, and reveals that China has a determined methodology in its espionage efforts. Such activity is a threat to the US national security and the reputation of the companies doing contract work for the US government. It can also impact the US economic position in the world.

Such industrial espionage cases can cause serious damage to the contractor company in loss of revenue, loss of continued work with the government, damage to the company's reputation and the stability of its stock. Industrial espionage in some cases can create a situation where a company will close its doors.

Another noteworthy case was that of Jonathan Pollard. Pollard was a civilian American Naval intelligence analyst working at the Naval Intelligence Command (NIC-1 Building) in Suitland, Maryland in the mid 1980s. I was assigned as a Naval Intelligence Officer in the NIC-1 building at that same time.

Pollard's rationalization for his espionage was that he discovered that information vital to Israel's security was being deliberately withheld by certain elements within the US national security establishment. His espionage was justified in his mind because he believed that Israel was legally entitled to this vital security information according to a 1983 Memorandum of Understanding between the two countries.

Jonathan Pollard was an ideologue, not a mercenary. This is based on a nine-month FBI investigation that concluded that Jonathan Pollard acted for ideological reasons only, not for money or any type of profit. This fact was recognized by the sentencing judge who declined to fine Pollard in addition to the jail sentence.

In 1985, when Jonathan Pollard's espionage activity was discovered by the United States government, his instructions from Israel were to seek refuge in the Israeli embassy in Washington, DC. When Pollard and his former wife sought refuge at the embassy, they were at first received, but then turned over to the FBI.

Jonathan Pollard never had a trial. At the request of both the United States and Israeli governments, he entered into a plea agreement, which spared both governments a long, difficult, expensive and potentially embarrassing trial. Pollard received a life sentence and a recommendation that he never be paroled. On May 11, 1998, Israel formally acknowledged Jonathan Pollard had been a bona fide Israeli agent.

These cases are examples of the threats to United States classified information. Such acts of espionage can target US military and government facilities, but also private industry working on government classified contracts. It is for that reason that private industry working with government classified information must follow the entire security mandated procedures related to such information. The US government security requirements related to the protection of classified information can be utilized in part for the protection of company confidential and protected information.

Defense Security Service

The Defense Security Service (DSS) is an agency of the Department of Defense (DoD) located in Quantico, Virginia with field offices throughout the United States. The Under Secretary of Defense for Intelligence provides authority, direction, and control over the DSS. The DSS provides the military services, defense agencies, twenty-four federal agencies and approximately 13,300 cleared contractor facilities, private industry, and universities, with security support services.

The DSS contributes to national security by serving as an interface between the government and cleared industry. DSS administers and implements the defense portion of the National Industrial Security Program pursuant to Executive Order 12829.

The Defense Security Service Center for Development of Security Excellence (CDSE) is located in Linthicum, Maryland and provides security education and training to DoD security professionals through formal classroom and distributed learning methodologies.

The Defense Industrial Security Clearance Office (DISCO) located in Fort Meade, Maryland, processes requests for industrial personnel security investigations and provides eligibility or clearance determinations for cleared industry personnel.

Industry Programs Partnership with Industry

The DSS Partnership with Industry Program (PWI) provides an opportunity for Industry and DSS industrial security professionals to work together in the protection of classified information. The goal of the program is for the participants to gain a mutual understanding of their respective roles in industrial security and to develop a better understanding and appreciation for the challenges and obstacles faced on both sides.

Participating industry professionals spend three to four days at a DSS site, normally a field or regional office. They work closely with DSS employees and gain a deeper understanding of how the DSS operates, the scope of the mission, upcoming initiatives, and the challenges faced by DSS in its oversight of the National Industrial Security Program.

DSS personnel spend three to four days participating in the program to gain exposure to issues faced by industry and to witness first-hand how security is integrated into a facility's day-to-day mission, how resources are allocated, and how industry security professionals balance internal business requirements with requirements from DSS and their GCAs.

The Defense Security Service Vision and Mission

Vision

To be the focal point of interaction and premier provider of industrial security and education services for the US government and the companies in the National Industrial Security Program in support of national security.

Mission

On behalf of the Department of Defense and other US government departments and agencies, the DSS supports national security and the war fighter through our security oversight and education missions. DSS oversees the protection of US and foreign classified information and technologies in the hands of industry under the National Industrial Security Program (NISP) and serves as the functional manager for the DoD security professional development program. We provide security education, training, and professional development services as the functional manager for the DoD security professional development program, and for other U.S. Government personnel and contractor employees, and representatives of foreign governments, as required.

Classification of US Government Information

Protected information related to the United States government is classified into three categories. This information may be developed by US government agencies, the military or private contractors and universities working on government projects as contractors. Regardless of whether it is developed by, utilized or stored by US government agencies, the military or private contractors and universities, if it is US government classified information, all organizations must follow the protection requirements.

Top secret: Information or material whose unauthorized disclosure could be expected to cause exceptionally grave damage to the national security.

Secret: Information or material whose unauthorized disclosure could be expected to cause serious damage to the national security.

Confidential: Information or material whose unauthorized disclosure could be expected to cause damage to the national security.

Information concerning the other categories of classified information that require special access authorization will be provided by the customer. These are the Sensitive Compartmented Information (SCI) or Special Access Program (SAP). For Official Use Only (FOUO) is unclassified DoD information which is exempt from general public disclosure and must not be given general circulation. Information concerning these classifications is used and held by private industry working in government security research, development, and production.

National Industrial Security Program Operating Manual

The National Industrial Security Program Operating Manual (NISPOM) is the US government's program designed to safeguard classified information that has been entrusted to private industry working via US government defense contracts. It is a three-way partnership in which the government customer or user agency enters into a classified contractual agreement with a cleared industrial facility and the DSS oversees and validates compliance with security portions of the contract the government has established. The following information

Figure 5.2 US Government classified document cover sheets for top secret, secret and confidential information. (Photo by Daniel J. Benny).

concerning the National Industrial Security Program Operating Manual was obtained from the National Counterintelligence Center 2011 Annual Report to Congress on Foreign Economic Collection and Industrial Espionage.

The National Industrial Security Program Operating Manual, established by Executive Order 12829 dated 06 January 1993, is industry's primary reference in the protection of classified information. The manual outlines the proper procedures for handling and safeguarding information classified pursuant to Executive Order 12958.

The program is administered within each cleared facility by the Facility Security Officer The Facility Security Officer office is responsible for all security matters relative to the safeguarding and handling of classified information.

Classified information is official government information that has been determined to require protection in the interest of national security. All classified information is under sole ownership of the United States government, and as such employees possess no right, interest, title, or claim to such information. The exception would be if the information was developed under an independent research and development program.

Classified information can be in many forms. It may be a piece of hardware, a photograph, a film, recording tapes, notes, a drawing, a document or spoken words. Classified material is marked as such upon origination. The protection required for the information safeguarding depends on its classification category. Three levels have been established based on their criticality to national interests as previously stated: top secret, secret, and confidential as well as Sensitive Compartmented Information (SCI), or Special Access Program (SAP). Official Use Only (FOUO) was also previously identified.

Marking Classified Information

All classified material must be conspicuously marked, stamped, or typed to show the level of its classification at the top and bottom of each page, front and back, and include the date of origin, and the name and address of the facility responsible for its preparation,. Each portion, section, part, paragraph, or similar portions of a classified document shall be marked to show the level of classification.

Physically marking classified information with appropriate classification and control markings serves to warn and inform holders of the degree of protection required. Other notations aid in derivative classification actions and facilitate downgrading or declassification. It is important that all classified information and material be marked to clearly convey the level of classification assigned the portions that contain or reveal classified information, the period of time protection is required, and any other notations required for protection of the information or material.

The following is taken from the NISPOM and is a summary of the most commonly used document control markings. More detailed information is available via the Internet from a variety of sources.[*]

---

[*] Classification and control markings and country designators authorized for use by the Intelligence Community are compiled in the Authorized Classification and Control Markings Register maintained by the DNI Special Security Center, Controlled Access Program Coordination Office (CAPCO).

Overall Classification Markings

The overall (i.e., highest) classification of a document is marked at the top and bottom of the outside cover (if there is one), the title page (if there is one), the first page, and the outside of the back cover (if there is one) or back side of the last page.

Each interior page containing classified information is marked top and bottom with the overall (i.e., highest) classification of the page. Each unclassified interior page is marked "Unclassified" at the top and bottom. Interior pages that are For Official Use Only need to be marked only at the bottom. Blank pages require no markings. Attachments and annexes may become separated from the basic document. They should be marked as if they were separate documents.

Additionally, every classified document must show, on the face of the document, the agency and office that created it and the date of creation. This information must be clear enough to allow someone receiving the document to contact the preparing office if questions or problems about classification arise.

US documents that contain foreign government information shall be marked on the front, "THIS DOCUMENT CONTAINS FOREIGN GOVERNMENT (indicate level) INFORMATION."

Computer files must be marked with appropriate headers and footers to ensure that anything that is transmitted or printed will have the applicable classification and associated markings. All removable storage media and devices such as diskettes, CD-ROMs, cassettes, magnet tape reels, etc., must have an outer label with the appropriate markings.

Each slide must be marked on the slide itself or slide cover, as well as on the image that is projected.

Automated Information Processing Requirements

Use of automated information systems to route and control access to information requires standard procedures for how documents are marked. Classification and control markings must follow a specified format that enables automated systems to recognize the markings.

Any classified document, either in hard copy or automated, must contain a header and footer with the classification, any control markings, and declassification date or designation. These three elements—classification, control marking(s), and declassification date—must be separated by two forward slashes and no spaces. If multiple dissemination control markings are used, they are separated by a comma and no spaces, except that multiple SCI controls are separated by a single forward slash and no spaces. Declassification date must be marked by an eight-digit number (year, month, day), exemption category (such as X1), or as Manual Review (MR). This is illustrated by the following examples:

SECRET//SI/TK//NOFORN//X1
SECRET//ORCON,PROPIN//20091231

A control marking such as FOR OFFICIAL USE ONLY cannot stand alone. It must be preceded by a classification as in:

UNCLASSIFIED//FOR OFFICIAL USE ONLY

When marking foreign government classified information, the classification is preceded by two forward slashes and countries are identified by an approved three-letter designator, as in//NATO SECRET or//DEU SECRET for Germany.

Portion Marking

The title or subject of a classified document is marked with the appropriate classification abbreviation in parentheses—(TS), (S), (C), or (U) immediately following and to the right of the title or subject. All documents containing information that requires control markings, regardless of classification, format, or medium, shall be portion marked. The overall classification of a document is equal to the highest classification level of any one portion found in the document.

Each portion of a classified document is to be marked with the appropriate classification abbreviation in parentheses immediately before the beginning of the portion. If the portion is numbered or lettered, place the abbreviation in parentheses between the letter or number and the start of the text. A portion is ordinarily defined as a paragraph, but also includes subjects, titles, graphics, tables, charts, bullet statements, sub-paragraphs, classified signature blocks, bullets, and other portions with slide presentations and the like.

Portions of US documents containing foreign government information are marked to reflect the foreign country of origin as well as
the appropriate classification, for example, (UK-C). Portions of US
documents containing extracts from NATO documents are marked
to reflect "NATO" or "COSMIC" as well as the appropriate classification; for example, (NATO-S) or (COSMIC-TS). Further information is available at Foreign Government Classified Information.

Point of Contact Marking

All intelligence reports shall include an intelligence community point
of contact and contact instructions at the end of the report. This is
required to expedite decisions on the sharing of the report.

Release to Foreign Countries/Organizations

In support of homeland security and coalition warfare, the US government has an increased need to share data with foreign countries,
international organizations, and multinational forces. This has led
to recent changes in the use of the "Released to..." (REL TO) control marking. This marking was previously only for use on intelligence information, but it is now authorized for use on all classified
defense information.

Following the REL TO marking is a list of countries to which the
information may be released through proper disclosure channels to
specified foreign governments or international organizations. This list
starts with USA and is followed by other countries listed alphabeti-
cally by the approved country code(s), international organization, or
coalition force.

Example: TOP SECRET//REL TO USA, EGY and ISR.

Access and Need to Know

Access to classified information occurs when a person has the legal
authority, ability, and opportunity to obtain knowledge of classified information. Authorized access to classified information may
be granted only when two conditions are met. First, the recipient

must have a valid and current security clearance at a level at least as high as the information to be released. Second, the recipient must demonstrate the need for access to the classified information. This is referred to as need to know. This means that access to that classified information is essential to the performance of his or her duties. It is the responsibility of the possessor of classified information to ensure the proper clearance and need to know of the recipient. Before the information is shared need to know confirmation must come from a security department or facility security officer.

Protection of Classified Information When in Use

When in use, classified material must never be left unsecured or unattended. It must be kept under constant surveillance by an authorized individual who is able to exercise direct control over the classified material. The authorized individual must have the appropriate clearance and need to know, and must take action to prevent access to the material when others who do not have the appropriate clearance and need to know are present.

Protection of Classified Information When in Storage

Classified information that is in storage must be secured in an approved security container. The storage of classified material in anything other than an approved container is strictly prohibited and the container must be locked. When opening a classified container, it should be shielded from sight so that the combination number cannot be observed.

The combinations to classified storage containers are classified and must be protected at the same level as the data they are protecting. Combinations to classified containers must be committed to memory and never written down.

Destruction of Classified Information

When it is determined that classified information is no longer required, it should be destroyed. Material to be destroyed must be entered on a destruction report and destroyed in a proper manner as required by the Defense Security Service.

Methods of Destruction of Classified Information

Classified documents and material need to be destroyed by burning, melting, chemical decomposition, pulping, pulverizing, cross-cut shredding, or mutilation sufficient to preclude recognition or reconstruction of the classified information. Burning is the preferred method of destroying classified information as it results in total destruction of the documents.

Procedures for destruction need to ensure that all classified information intended for destruction actually needs to be established. Destruction records and utilizing the two-person rule, that is, having two cleared persons involved in the entire destruction process, will satisfy this requirement for top secret information. Imposition of a two-person rule, without destruction records, will satisfy this requirement for secret information, as will use of destruction records without imposition of the two-person rule.

Burn bags are used for the collection of classified material that is to be destroyed at central destruction facilities. Those bags must be controlled in a manner designed to minimize the possibility of their unauthorized removal and the unauthorized removal of their classified contents prior to actual destruction. When filled, burn bags must be sealed in a manner to insure the detection of any tampering with the bag.

Procedures must also be established to ensure that all classified information intended for destruction actually is destroyed. Records of destruction are required for top secret information. The record shall be dated and signed at the time of destruction by two persons cleared for access to top secret information. Records of the destruction of secret and confidential data must be maintained.

Transmitting Classified Information

The transmitting of classified information will be performed by the facility security officer. Methods for transmittal of classified information depend on the material's classification and its destination. The facility security officer must insure that the material is properly packaged and transmitted in accordance with the NISPOM.

Reproducing Classified Material

Classified information that needs to be reproduced must be cleared with the facility security officer. Each copy made must be documented into the organization's information management system. Only approved copying machines must be utilized for the reproduction of classified information.

Suspicious Espionage Activity

Employees are required to report any suspicious behavior or occurrences that may occur at any time related to possible espionage of classified information. Incidents must be reported to the facility security officer. Suspicious activity would include: Efforts, to obtain illegal or unauthorized access to classified or sensitive information, efforts to compromise a cleared employee who could be turned for espionage, contact by a cleared employee with a known or suspected intelligence officer from any country, or contact where the employee concerned may be the target of any attempted exploitation by the intelligence services of another country.

Cleared Employee Reporting Requirements

Cleared employees are required to report information related to the following situations to the facility security officer:

- Foreign travel to or through a country that is overtly hostile to the US or attendance at international conferences at which representatives of such a country were or will be in attendance.
- The establishment of residency in an overtly hostile country by an employee's spouse or member of his/her immediate family, or the acquisition of relatives, through marriage, who live in such a country, must be reported.

- If there is any loss, compromise, or suspected compromise of classified information in your possession or in the possession of another person.
- Any association with or intention to represent a foreign interest is also reportable.
- Change in name, residence, or marital status.
- Any instances in which classified material is out of the control of the custodian or which cannot be readily located.
- Any instances in which someone is approached and requests information pertaining to classified information when such person does not have a legitimate need to know and/or is willing to pay money for such information.
- Serious financial problems or law suits need to be reported.
- Acts of sabotage or possible sabotage, espionage or attempted espionage, and any subversive or suspicious activity are critical and must be reported to security and or law enforcement at once.

Check List of What to Report

Contractor/company must report events that affect:

- Status of facility clearance
- Status of employee's personnel security clearance
- Proper safeguarding of classified information
- Indication of classified information loss or compromise

Contactors/company must specifically report:

- Security violations
- Suspicious contacts

Indications of:

- Espionage
- Sabotage
- Terrorism
- Subversive activity

To Whom to Report

- Facility security officer (FSO)
- DSS industrial security representative (IS Rep)
- DSS counterintelligence (CI) specialist

Departure of Cleared Employees

All cleared employees have a responsibility to surrender all classified material in their possession to the facility security officer upon termination. The employee must be "read out" and sign a debriefing form return company keys, access cards, and identification prior to departure.

Required Security Briefing

The National Industrial Security Program Operating Manual requires that before one is granted access to classified information, he or she must receive and an initial security briefing and an additional refresher security training annually. The training must include threat awareness, an overview of the security classification system, and employee reporting obligations and requirements.

Manual for Physical Security Standards for Sensitive Compartmented Information

Some private organizations may be under government contract to work with special sensitive information. The Director of Central Intelligence Directive 1/21 Manual for Physical Security Standards for Sensitive Compartmented Information covers the requirements for the protection of sensitive compartmented information (SCI). This information is so sensitive that the protection measures applied to top secret information are not sufficient. The area in which this is formation is stored and work with is called a sensitive compartmented information facility (SCIF). It is a specially created area, room or facility designed for the handling, discussion, access, control and storage of top secret sensitive compartmented information (TS/SCI).

The design of this facility needs to meet the requirement of Director of Central Intelligence Directive 1/21 Manual for Physical Security

Standards for Sensitive Compartmented Information Facilities and consider the threats and vulnerabilities of espionage. The requirements of the manual cover access control, the intrusion detection systems, communication, storage of the protected material and control of the material when it is being worked on within SCIFs.

Compartmented Information Facility

With regard to access control, there needs to be only one access point. When in operation access needs to be controlled by security, only authorized individuals may enter upon showing photo identification. Authorized visitors may have access but must sign in and be escorted at all times.

The facility cannot have any windows. Walls, ceilings, and floor must be of solid construction. When not occupied, the facility must be completely protected within an intrusion detection system and a timely security response to any alarms.

No personal communications or recording devices are permitted into the SCIF. All landline telephone and communications must be encrypted. A white noise generator will also be employed. This device broadcasts a continuous low level multi-frequency audio sound which masks voices making eavesdropping near to impossible.

Duct work within the SCIF must be limited in size and protected with heavy gauge grills over all openings. The ducts also need to be baffled to prevent the monitoring of sound from the outside through the ductwork. Vibration detector sensors can be placed in the ducts to identify anyone attempting to gain access through the ductwork and utility ports.

All the SCI/TC information must be secured in security vaults when not in use. An inventory of all SCI/TS material used during the work shift must all be made to ensure all information is accounted for.

Personnel controls must be established. Access rosters listing all persons authorized access to the facility shall be maintained at the SCIF point of entry. Electronic systems, including coded security identification cards or badges may be used in lieu of security access rosters. Visitor identification and control: each SCIF shall have procedures for identification and control of visitors seeking access to the SCIF.

The US government classification system and protection requirements that have been discussed have been established to provide for the safekeeping of all documents.

Bibliography

Association of Certified Fraud Examiners (2000). *Corporate Espionage*. Austin, TX: Association of Certified Fraud Examiners.

Baker, P. & Benny, D. J. (2012). *Complete Guide to Physical Security*. Boca Raton, FL: CRC Press.

Central Intelligence Agency (2012). *Factbook*. Washington, DC: US Government Printing Office.

Defense Security Service (2013). Retrieved from http://www.dss.mil/

Director of Central Intelligence Directive 1/21 Manual for Physical Security Standards for Sensitive Compartmented Information Facilities (1994). Washington, DC: US Government Printing Office.

Fischer, R. J. & Green, G. (2004). *Introduction to Security* (7th ed). Burlington, MA: Elsevier.

Heims, P. (1982). *Countering Industrial Espionage*. Surrey, UK: 20th Century Security Education.

Johnson, W.M. (2007). *Business Espionage*. Shoreline, WA: Questor Group.

Martin, S. (2005). *Business Intelligence and Corporate Espionage*. Boston, MA: Pearson.

The National Counterintelligence Center (2011). Annual Report to Congress on Foreign Economic Collection and Industrial Espionage. Washington, DC: US Government Printing Office.

Office of National Intelligence (2013). Retrieved from http://www.intelligence.gov/about-the-intelligence-community

Richelson, J. T. (1999). *The US Intelligence Community*. Boulder, CO: Westview Press.

Heims, P. (1982). *Countering Industrial Espionage*. Surrey, UK: 20th Century Security Education.

Winker, I. (1997). *Corporate Espionage*. New York, NY: Prima Publishing.

6
Physical Security

Physical security measures need to be utilized as part of a comprehensive counterespionage program. Physical security will aid in the protection of both life and sensitive information. The physical security sensors described in this chapter include both current and older technology. Older security sensors and systems are discussed because they may still be found at some locations and they can still be utilized as part of a total security system. If there are upgrades to the system and/or new construction, the most current technology security sensors and system should be utilized.

The goals of physical security are to:

- Deter entry by the use of signs, intrusion detection systems, barriers, locks, access control, metal detectors, x-ray and security cameras; physical security can deter an individual from taking part in espionage activity.
- Delay entry by utilizing various physical security measures. Should an individual not be deterred and attempt to take part in criminal activity and industrial espionage, the physical security measures can delay the perpetrator. During this period of delay, the perpetrator may be observed by a security officer, staff, or local law enforcement and the crime can be averted.
- Detect entry with the use of physical security devices. Should an individual attempt to take part in criminal activity his or her presence and actions will be detected. This could result in the perpetrator stopping the criminal activity. It could result in the detection by security officers, or staff and apprehension by law enforcement. If a crime or the loss of a company's confidential information is detected, management knows that there has been a threat and can evaluate the adequacy of the current physical security system to prevent future threats.

- Physical security also controls the movement of people such as employees, visitors, researchers and vendors. Physical security measures can control individuals entering and leaving the property and access to secured areas. Physical security also controls the movement of vehicles entering the property. These may be vehicles owned or driven by employees, visitors, researchers or vendors.

Intrusion Detections System

An intrusion detection system is designed to provide notice of someone entering a protected area. This is accomplished by a system of sensors that sends a notification to the computer base's monitoring stations or to a local sound producing device when the sensor is activated. The intrusion detection system can be a proprietary central station monitored by security. It can also be a contract central station. The contract central station is a contract service not located or associated with the property being protected. The contract central station receives the alarm and then notifies police, fire, emergency medical services, and the property security on the type of alarm that is received.

The most commonly utilized sensors include:

Electromagnetic contacts
Photoelectric
Laser
Glass breakage
Pressure
Vibration
Audio
Ultrasonic
Microwave
Passive infrared
Capacitance proximity

Electromagnetic Contacts

Electromagnetic contacts are used to provide protection for doors and windows. Contacts are placed on the door and door frame or the

Figure 6.1   Electromagnetic sensor. (Photo by Dr. Daniel J. Benny)

window and window sash. When the door or window is closed, the contacts match together. When the alarm system is activated, a current passes through the matching contacts. When the door or window is opened while the alarm is activated it breaks the circuit and the alarm is activated (see Figure 6.1).

Photoelectric

This sensor is utilized to protect doors and passageways or an entrance to a sensitive area and is based on the principle of the use of a light beam. When the light beam is broken by an individual, the alarm is activated. While they are no used any longer they may be found in old security systems. The photoelectric cell can also be used to automatically activate security lighting during periods of darkness.

Laser

The laser sensor can protect doors and passageways and is based on the use of a laser light beam. When the laser beam is broken, the alarm is activated. It can also be used to automatically activate security lighting during periods of darkness.

Glass Breakage

This sensor is used on glass windows or door areas with glass to detect attempted entry through the breaking of glass. The sensor is mounted on the glass itself or near the glass window or door glass area and detects the vibration of the breaking glass.

Pressure-Sensitive Sensor

The pressure-sensitive sensor is used to detect a person walking on a surface in the interior of a structure or on the exterior grounds. The sensor is placed under the carpet inside of a property. If used outdoors, it is buried under the surface of the ground when used. The alarm is activated when an individual walks over the surface where the sensor is concealed.

Vibration

This is used to provide protection in utility ports large enough to be accessed by an individual. When a perpetrator attempts to access an area protected by this sensor and touches the vibration sensor, the alarm is activated.

Audio

The audio sensor is a microphone and, in most cases, a series of microphones placed inside the facility to be protected. Should there be an unauthorized access into the structure, the microphones are activated and transmit all sounds to a central station monitored by the property security department or a contract central station. The security officer can then dispatch a response and notify the local police.

Ultrasonic

The ultrasonic sensor is used to protect the interior of an unoccupied facility. The sensor transceiver sends out sonar waves across the room that transverse back to the transceiver in a timed sequence. Should a perpetrator enter the protected area, the sonar waves are interrupted and the alarm is activated. This system is not recommended for hangars because the air movement that can occur can set off the alarm.

Microwave

This sensor is also used to protect the interior of an unoccupied facility. The sensor transceiver sends out microwaves across the room that traverse back to the transceiver in a timed sequence. Should a perpetrator enter the protected area, the microwaves are interrupted and the alarm is activated. This sensor should not be used in a room with large areas of glass as it will penetrate the glass and could result in false alarms. It may also be use to protect outdoor areas with restricted access (see Figure 6.2).

Passive Infrared

The passive infrared sensor is the best motion transceiver for use in the interior protection of an unoccupied facility (see Figure 6.3). The sensor transceiver sends out light energy that detects body heat. Should a perpetrator enter the protected area, the passive infrared detects the

Figure 6.2   Microwave on the White House lawn, Washington, DC. (Photo by Daniel J. Benny)

Figure 6.3 Passive infrared. (Photo by Daniel J. Benny)

intruder's body heat and the heat in the protected area and activates the alarm. This sensor is recommended.

Capacitance Proximity

This sensor is designed to protect metal safes and metal security containers. Once the sensor is attached to the metal safe or metal security container, a magnetic field is established. The magnetic field extends one foot around the protected safe or container. When a person walks into that space or touches the safe or container, the intruder's body interrupts the magnetic field protecting the safe or security container and activates the alarm. This may be used for a safe or steel key security container.

Nearly all protection systems now include intrusion detection and fire safety in one integrated system. The fire protection system can be activated manually by use of a pull station should one smell or see smoke and fire. The pull station activates the audio and visual strobes, the fire protection enunciators in the building, and notifies the central station and/or emergency dispatch for the fire department. In addition to the manual pull station, there is a fire protection sensor that can be placed in the protected facility that will send an automatic signal to the central station and or emergency dispatch for the fire department and activate a set of the audible and visual strobe fire protection enunciators.

The following fire protection sensors will be utilized:

Duel chamber smoke detector
Rate of rise heat detector
Natural gas or carbon monoxide detectors
Water flow
Security cameras

Dual Chamber Smoke Detector

This sensor provides early smoke detection. It is used primarily for the protection of life, but the early detection of a fire can also save property (Figure 6.4).

Rate of Rise Heat Detector

This sensor is used in areas where a smoke detector cannot be used. These include bathrooms and cooking areas, and cultural property repair shops where the normal activity in those areas would set off a

Figure 6.4   Dual chamber smoke detector. (Photo by Daniel J. Benny)

smoke detector. The rate of rise heat detector senses a rapid increase of heat in an area due to a fire and activates the alarm system.

Natural Gas or Carbon Monoxide Detectors

These two sensors are used to detect deadly gases that may build up in a facility and provide early warning for evacuation.

Water Flow

For facilities that have fire protection sprinkler systems, this sensor detects the drop in water pressure when the sprinkler is activated during a fire. This results in an alarm being activated.

Security Cameras

The use of security camera surveillance at museums, historic sites, archives or libraries is very effective in the prevention of crime. It also allows the documentation of events and provides evidence for an investigation should a crime occur. Security cameras can be utilized to provide protection from both external and internal theft (see Figures 6.5 and 6.6).

Figure 6.5   Interior security camera. (Photo of Daniel J. Benny)

Figure 6.6 Exterior security camera. (Photo by Daniel J. Benny)

Organizations may install security cameras at any location on the exterior of their property and in nearly all interior areas. The areas where a security camera may not be utilized are rest rooms and locker rooms. Other than those locations, there is no expectation of privacy in the workplace. Key areas for the placement of security cameras include entrances and exits to all property buildings and coverage of areas where sensitive information is stored. There should be outdoor coverage of parking areas and the grounds of the property by security cameras.

The components of a security camera system include the lens/camera, transmission of the signal, monitoring, and recording.

Lens/Camera   An effective security camera requires a low light and a variable lens so that it is adaptable to low light situations. This is critical for security coverage inside galleries and exhibit areas. This will allow effective operations during both day and night hours. The camera should be color rather than black and white in order to identify color that is critical in security applications. It should be housed in a protective cover and have the ability to be operated remotely to allow for zoom, pan and tilt.

Transmission of the Signal   Methods of transmitting the signal include the use of coaxial cable, fiber optics, the Ethernet, microwave, radio frequency, and laser. The best connection would be from coaxial cable, fiber optics or the Ethernet. In situations where a direct line cannot be used due to distance or other factors, microwave, radio frequency, and laser can be used.

Monitoring   The camera image can be viewed on a tradition television screen that should have a resolution of no less than 512–491 pixels with 580 lines. It can also be viewed on a desktop or laptop computer screens.

Digital Recording and Monitoring   This can be accomplished by use of a digital recording system. Digital recording allows for the ability to store more information for a longer period of time depending on the server's capacity. It also allows obtaining stills from the video and enhancing and enlarging them for identification and to share with law enforcement agencies. Another important feature of digital recording is that a time frame in the video can be searched by typing in the date and time period. This makes retrieving and reviewing an important time event fast and easy. Recordings can also be monitored remotely on a laptop computer (see Figure 6.7).

Figure 6.7   Laptop computer used to monitor digital security cameras. (Photo by Daniel J. Benny)

Motion Detection   Security cameras can be equipped to work in conjunction with motion detection sensors that activate the recording of the view
of the camera only during the time of the activation by the motion sensor.
The advantage is that this reduces the amount of recorded time on a VHS
tape when using the analog system or space on the server when using the
digital system. It is most often used during the investigation of internal
theft when the security department only needs to view an area when the
sensor has been activated rather than going through hours of recordings.

Determining Total System Cost

When determining the total security system cost there are several
categories that must be explored. These include:

- System design cost
- System installation cost
- System operational cost
- Maintenance cost
- IT cost
  - Replacement cost
  - Return on investment

It is important to determine the total cost of the system in order to
develop a realistic budget that can be justified to top management and
to ensure that the system that is installed meets the security requirements of the organization based on the threat.

System Design Cost

Initially, there is the cost of developing the specifications for the project. This phase may require the assistance of a security consultant or
an engineer, depending on the complexity and sophistication of the
total security system.

The examination of these requirements includes the type of security system that would be the most effective based on the threat, the
location being protected, and the various components of the system.
The system components include the intrusion detection system central station server, the computer to be utilized to operate the security
system, and the monitors that will be required to work the system.

Depending on the size and number of monitors, a rack system may have to be constructed to hold the monitors.

The various types, numbers, and placement of the security sensors will need to be determined and documented. As an example, the system could include electronic door contacts or passive inferred sensors. The number and placement of fire sensors could include smoke detectors, heat detectors, and water flow sensors and would need to be determined.

Access controls such as card readers, cyber locks and traditional locks and their placement in the facility must be identified. If electronic access control devices are utilized, conduit and wiring to power the units will need to be calculated into the cost of the project.

The number and operating requirements of the security cameras will need to be identified including the type of lens and the camera body as well as operating aspects such as zoom capabilities and transmission method. Conduit and wiring necessary to power the units will also need to be calculated.

The design cost will include development of the drawings and blueprints of the total system to be constructed and installed. There are, of course, consultant fees for the individual or firm hired to design the security system along with the cost of the engineer or engineering firm who will create the drawing and blueprints of the project.

Many aspects of the system design cost must be taken into account. This will be important when submitting the budget. The life cycle of the security system should also be a consideration for long-term budget projection.

System Installation Cost

One of the most expensive aspects of the entire security system project will be the cost of installation. This includes the cost of the products or components of the security system and will include:

- Server
- Computer
- Monitors
- Control panel
- Wiring

- Metal conduit
- Security cameras
- Camera brackets and housing

Also to be included will be the expense of the various sensors such as door and window contacts, motion sensors, and fire protection sensors integrated into the system. If access control is part of the system, there is the cost of the readers and cards to be used with the product.

In addition, once the products have been identified and purchased, there will be the shipping cost to transport the system components to the installation site. This could include fees for rail and truck transport of large parts and the cost of local carriers for smaller products associated with the security system.

Labor costs for the individuals installing the system can be sizeable based on the local union or non-union wages in the local area. This cost would include electricians and other construction workers needed to support the security system. It may also include masons, carpenters and painters.

Permits will be required from the local government or municipality in most cases for the new construction and electrical installations. The cost of the permits will vary based on the local governments and their specific requirements. Based on the nature of the product, there may also be state or Environmental Protection Agency permit fees to pay.

System Operational Cost

Once the system is installed, there will be initial and ongoing system operation costs. In order to insure the proper function of the system, current policies will need to be rewritten and new policies will need to be written with regard to the security system's operation. These operational changes may impact how other departments in the organization operate and making those changes may result in additional cost.

Since all new security systems are computer-based, significant initial and ongoing support will be required from the organization's IT department. This includes integrating the security system into the company's IT system, the development of IT security procedures, and software to protect the system.

The increase in cost for electrical power is also part of the system operating cost and in the event of a power loss, the security system must function. To prevent a power loss, an emergency backup generator must be included in the ongoing cost.

The most expensive ongoing cost will be the initial and continued training of the security staff and the wages for additional security staff that will monitor the security system. In some cases, the addition of a comprehensive security system may free some security officers on patrol to monitor the system, but this is not the norm. In most situations, additional security will need to be hired.

IT Related Cost

When developing a new computer-based security system, there will be IT related cost. It is vital to know what IT systems are available on the corporate IP network. In the total coast of the security system you will need to account for the cost factors associated with industry best practices for the management of IP-based technologies such as:

- Antivirus technology
- System patches
- Database management
- Backup and archiving
- Network bandwidth and quality of service

Each of these will have associated cost for labor and the IT personnel who may be dedicated partially or fully to monitoring and maintaining the new systems.

Maintenance Cost Keeping the system operating will require an investment in ongoing maintenance, which would include routine costs to keep the system hardware running and upgrades to the software. It will also require updates to the physical components of the system such as wiring and mechanical functions.

If the system goes down in an emergency situation, there will be emergency repair and labor costs, especially during the evening, weekends or holidays when labor rates are higher. There will also be the labor cost for additional security and management staff to provide security coverage if the security system is not operating.

One method of reducing routine and emergency labor costs is to enter into an annual maintenance contract. It often allows a reduced rate for monthly or quarterly work on the security system, as well as emergency maintenance situations during the day, evenings, weekends or holidays.

Replacement cost   All things may pass and that is true of security systems that become inoperable or antiquated. When designing and installing a new system, it is important to determine the life of the system. How long will it last before it needs to be replaced or becomes obsolete based on new hardware or software?

The manufacturer can most often advise on the life cycle of the system and potential future changes that may occur along with a time frame for such changes. Based on the life expectancy projection, a long-term budget should be established so that there are funds for the replacement of the security system at the anticipated replacement time. The life cycle of the security system should also be a consideration when a system is first selected.

Cost–Benefit Analysis   When developing a security system, stakeholders must often prioritize requirements as part of the engineering process. Not all aspects may be implemented due to lack of time, resources, or changing or unclear project goals. It is important to define which requirements should be given priority over others.

Cost of Loss   Computing the cost of a security system can be very difficult. A simple cost calculation can take into account the cost of repairing or replacing the security system. A more sophisticated cost calculation can consider the cost of having security system out of service, added training, additional procedures resulting from a loss, the cost to a company's reputation, and clients. For most purposes, you do not need to assign an exact value to each possible risk. Normally, assigning a cost range to each item is sufficient.

The following is one method to analyze the cost is to assign these costs based on a scale of loss:

Non-availability of security systems over a short term (7–10 days)
Non-availability of security system over a medium term (1–2 weeks)

Non-availability of security system over a long term (more than
  2 weeks)
Permanent loss or destruction of the security system
Accidental partial loss or damage of the security system
Deliberate partial loss or damage of the security system
Unauthorized disclosure within the organization
Replacement or recovery cost of the security system

The Cost of Prevention

Calculating the cost of preventing each type of loss could include the
cost to recover from:

- Fire
- Power failure
- Terrorist incident

Costs need to be amortized over the expected lifetime of the security system.

Return on Investment (ROI)

In all areas of management including the development of a total security system, return on investment (ROI) is a critical step in selling the
system to top management and obtaining funding for the project.

ROI is a concept used to maximize profit to an organization for
monies spent. It is used to determine the security system's financial worth. ROI is the annual rate of return on an investment. A
security investment such as a physical security system can enhance
the security picture and create an improved financial picture of the
organization. Many security professionals have the technical security knowledge to sell a security system to top management, but lack
the ability to show how security improvements can contribute to a
company's profitability.

When making the business case for a total security system investment that will include software or hardware, it is imperative to accu-
rately capture both the costs and the benefits, and to present the
results in compelling financial terms. Knowledge on how to quan-
tify the security investment and the projected return in ways that top

management and other financial stake holders are used to seeing can be critical to obtaining endorsement of the security system.

Return on investment can be measured using two basic criteria: costs and benefits. The object is to establish a credible ROI and also to define a high-value security system project by the benefits that it provides. It is important to capture all the relevant costs of a project as it relates to ROI.

It is also important to identify the purpose of the security system project. Is the project worth it? Will it improve security? If you can answer yes, the next decision is the priority of the security system project in the scheme of the total organizational goals. While security risk needs to be a priority, financial factors are a reality. Fiscally responsible planning and prioritizing will weigh in the project's favor in the decision-making process. The description of the project's purpose should include a clear statement for the need of the security system.

Total Cost of Ownership (TCO)

Total cost of ownership (TCO) is the cost to an organization to acquire, support, and maintain the security system. TCO can be articulated this way:

TCO = cost to buy + cost to install + cost to operate + cost to maintain

Cost Factor

Three are common cost factors associated with the development of a security system. It is vital to estimate both the extent and timing of costs to be incurred during the security systems project.

Typical cost factors for security systems may include the following:

Security and video cameras
    Cameras
    Encoders
    Fiber transceivers
    Monitors for VCR-DVR-NVR
    Mass storage access control panels

Doors and locks
   Reader
   Gates
   Other security sensors

Communications
   Leased line costs
   Cost associated with interoperability of systems
   Cabling and power supplies

Personnel associated with the security system
   Receptionist
   Credentialing
   Contractor administration
   Lock and key management

Monitoring and control rooms
   Alarm and video monitoring personnel
   Operations support personnel
   Physical security information management systems
   Awareness and response systems

General system-related costs
   Engineering and design
   Infrastructure and maintenance
   Software and licensing
   System deployment
   Application integration
   Administration and troubleshooting
   User training

To be successful in selling the project you must identify the benefits related to ROI. Start with the direct benefits, which are verifiable and easy to understand. Indirect benefits can be selectively included later if they contribute to the ROI.

The ROI can be justified based on the direct benefits attributable to the security system project. Direct benefits may include:

- Space improvements
- Wiring and communications infrastructure improvements
- Servers, applications, or systems improvements

- Storage increase
- Integration of systems such as security, fire protection, access control
- System maintenance and upgrades
- Training improvements

Indirect benefits are not easily measured. Productivity improvement is an example of an indirect benefit. Since indirect benefits may involve some subjectivity, separating indirect and direct benefits makes proposal evaluation easier, increasing its chances of receiving thorough consideration. IP-based physical security can be used to increase efficiency and provide labor reduction.

The following list is an example of indirect benefits:

- Visitor management administration and control
- Segregation of duties
- Parking permit administration
- Property pass administration
- Employee time keeping
- System troubleshooting and maintenance
- Alarm correlation and response
- Emergency communication and notification

Once the cost and benefit data are collected, they must be analyzed to determine the ROI. This can be accomplished by using the TCO comparisons as shown above. Presenting the ROI it should be done in a clear and concise executive summary.

Capturing this advantage in quantifiable and credible terms will permit the calculation of the ROI. In the current business climate, it is crucial to justify the expenditure of a security system even if the risk shows that it is vital to the security of the organization. Using the ROI model will demonstrate the security director's business acumen, sensitivity to resource limitations, and will build the security manager's credibility with top management.

Determining the total cost is an important aspect in the development of the proposed security system. It aids in gaining approval for the security system and the funding for the project by top management.

Locks, Key Control, and Access Control

The use of locks is one of the oldest forms of security. There are two general categories of locks; those that operate on mechanical concepts and those that use electricity to operate mechanical components of the locking system. Locks are used to secure personal doors, windows, utility ports, gates, file cabinets, and security containers in the protection of people, artifacts, books, and collections.

In addition to preventing access based on security concerns, locks can also prevent access to areas for safety related issues. This might include securing hazardous materials storage areas, electrical rooms, and to lock out equipment on/off switched.

Mechanical Locks   A mechanical lock utilizes physical moving parts and barriers to prevent the opening of the latch and includes the latch or bolt that holds the door or window to the frame. The strike is the part into which the latch is inserted. The barrier is a tumbler array that must be passed by use of a key to operate the latch. The key is used to pass through the tumbler array and operates the latch or bolt.

Wafer Tumbler Lock   This lock utilizes flat metal tumblers that function inside the shell of the lock housing and create a shear line. Spring tension keeps each wafer locked into the shell until lifted out by the key. The shell is matched by varying bit depths on the key.

Dial Combination Lock   The dial combination lock is used on security container, safes, and vaults and is opened by dialing in a set combination. By eliminating a keyway, it provides a higher level of security. While dial combination locks do not utilize a key, they work on the same principle as the lever lock. By aligning gates on tumblers to allow insertion of the fence in the bolt, the lock can be opened by dialing in the assigned combination. The number of tumblers in the lock will determine the numbers to be used to open the combination lock.

High Security Dead Bolt Lock   The dead bolt lock is utilized for securing exterior and interior doors (see Figure 6.8). The elements of high security dead bolt locks are the use of a restricted keyway so the key cannot be easily duplicated and a one-inch latch with ceramic inserts

Figure 6.8   Deadbolt lock. (Photo by Daniel J. Benny)

so the latch cannot be forced open or cut. Tapered and rotating cylinder guards should be used so that a wrench cannot remove the lock.

Card Access Electrified Locks   Electrified locks permit doors to be locked and unlocked in a remote manner (see Figure 9.9). An electrified lock can be a simple push button near the lock or at a security central station or work as part of a card reader system or digital keypad. This system allows for the use of traditional electric latches or can be used with an electric high security deadbolt system.

Exit Locks   Exit locks or panic bars are used on doors designed as emergency exits from a building (see Figure 6.10). They are locked from the outside, but can be opened to allow exiting the building by pushing on a bar that disengages the lock. Emergency doors are never to be locked from the inside in any manner that would not allow for immediate exit from the building.

Master Locking System   A master locking system must be designed to meet the security needs of an airport, fixed based operator, and/ or flight school. Without planning, the locking system will usually degrade to a system that is provides only privacy, not effective security.

Figure 6.9 Proximity card reader. (Photo by Daniel J. Benny)

The goal is to make the locking system effective and user friendly so that the functions of the facility can continue unimpeded.

The following design criteria to be considered in the development of a master locking system include the total number of locks that will be installed on exterior and interior doors. The categories of the locking system will include exterior doors entering the building on the property, interior doors, high security areas, combination locks for security containers and safes, and desk, computer and file cabinet locks.

Control of Keys and Locking Devices

The security department or the manager should control all keys and locking devices. This includes responsibility for the installation and repair of all locks, as well as maintaining the records of all keys made, issued, and collected.

Figure 6.10   Emergency door locking system. (Photo by Daniel J. Benny)

Master Key   The master key, a single key that fits all locks, must be controlled and secured by the security department or manager and should never be removed from the property. This key may be signed out to members of the staff. It should only be issued daily and should be signed for and returned at the end of every shift. Sub-master keys that allow access to specific areas of the airport may be issued for the term of employment to top management or security staff. The security department should keep a duplicate of all keys to the facility, desk, file cabinets and access numbers to combination locks on security containers.

Duplication of Keys   The duplication of keys company keys must be controlled. No key should be duplicated without the authorization of the management or the security department.

Lost Keys   Lost or misplaced keys are to be reported at once. An investigation in the circumstances related to the loss or misplacement of keys must be conducted.

Disposition of Employee Keys upon Transfer or Termination   Upon the transfer or the termination of an employee, all keys issued to that employee must be returned and accounted for. This includes door, desk, and file cabinet keys.

Security Containers

As discussed previously in Chapter 5, when protecting sensitive information it is vital to have the documents or media stored in security containers or safes. Some documents may require security, but may not be so sensitive that they require Class 1 to 3 containers. In these instances, Class 4 to 6 containers, classified as follows, may be used:

Class 4   The security container is not insulated and the protection provided is:

> 20 man-minutes against surreptitious entry
> 5 man-minutes against forced entry
> 20 man-hours against manipulation of the lock
> 20 man-hours against radiological attack

Class 5   The security container is not insulated and the protection provided is:

> 20 man-hours against surreptitious entry (increased from 30 man-minutes on containers produced after March 1991)
> 10 man-minutes against forced entry
> 20 man-hours against manipulation of the lock
> 20 man-hours against radiological attack
> 30 man-minutes against covert entry

Class 6   The security container is not insulated and the protection provided is:

> 20 man-hours against surreptitious entry

No forced entry test requirement
20 man-hours against manipulation of the lock
20 man-hours against radiological attack
30 man-minutes against covert entry

Security Filing Cabinets

A variety of security filing cabinets are manufactured to meet the standards of the Class 5 and Class 6 security containers. Security filing cabinets are available in a variety of styles to include single, two, four, and five drawers and in both letter size and legal size models.

Security Barriers and Fencing

A security barrier can be anything that prevents vehicle or pedestrian access to the property or the facility and protected information. Barriers may be natural such as water, trees, or rock formations. These natural barriers may already be in place or can be placed on the property (see Figure 6.11). A constructed water barrier may also be used (see Figure 6.12). This is one aspect of what is known as Crime Prevention through Environmental Design (CPTED).

Figure 6.11 Alcatraz Island, San Francisco, CA has water as a natural barrier. (Photo by Daniel J. Benny)

Figure 6.12   A Tudor estate in England protected by a water moat. (Photo by Daniel J. Benny)

One of the most cost-effective security barriers used to secure the perimeter of the property or high risk areas such as fueling tanks is a chain link fence (see Figure 6.13). Chain link fence is relatively inexpensive and provides the flexibility to move as needed. It also allows visibility beyond the property line by security, staff and security cameras.

Figure 6.13   Chain link fence, Daytona Beach, FL. (Photo by Daniel J. Benny)

Figure 6.14 Decorative fencing at White House gate, Washington, DC. (Photo by Daniel J. Benny)

Chain link fence may be used for some outdoor storage areas, but may not be appropriate at some facilities because it is not esthetically pleasing. Decorative fencing is often more esthetically appealing and can provide adequate perimeter security (see Figure 6.14).

If utilized, the security industry height for the fence is six feet with a one foot top guard mounted on a forty-five degree angle facing away from the property constructed of barbed wire and or razor ribbon. The fence must be secured in the ground by metal posts with bracing across the top and bottom of the fence. The opening in the fence should be no more than two inches.

With fencing that is utilized for areas requiring vehicle access, there should be at least two points of access in the event that one access is closed due to an emergency. All gates that are not used on a regular basis need to be secured with a high-security padlock. The locked gate should also be equipped with a numbered security seal. This seal needs to be checked each day by security or airport staff to ensure the numbered seal is intact and matches the numbered seal placed on the gate. This is to ensure that an unauthorized key is not used. It is also used to ensure that the original padlock on the gate was not was cut off and replaced with a different lock and then used by a perpetrator for continued unauthorized access into the secure area.

Access onto the property through the gate can be control by the use of a proximity access card and electric locking system on the gate. These can be used for vehicles or individuals.

Security Lighting

Security lighting is used to illuminate the perimeter of the property, gate access area, walkway, and the vehicle parking area of the facility. The most effective security lighting is the sodium vapor type (see Figure 6.15).

Lighting fixtures need to be placed in a security housing to prevent damage. The lights can be mounted on posts and buildings. Lights can be activated by the use of a photoelectric cell that automatically turns them on at dusk and off at dawn. This is more efficient than manually turning the lights on and off each day.

All light fixtures should be numbered and identified for easy identification. This will be of value when reporting lights that are not working because it will help ensure that they are repaired as quickly as possible.

Figure 6.15   Exterior security and emergency lighting. (Photo by Daniel J. Benny)

These types of lighting include the following:

- Incandescent
- New fluorescent (to replace the incandescent)
- Quartz
- Mercury vapor
- Sodium vapor

Incandescent   Known as the common light bulb or flood light, the incandescent bulb is being phased out. It has been used to provide illumination at doorways and to direct light to a building at night. It is suitable for security for a single building, but is not considered effective for security lighting of large facilities because of the high energy cost and low illumination that it provides.

New Fluorescent (To Replace Incandescent)   The new fluorescent lights provide illumination at doorways and direct light to a building at night and are replacing the incandescent bulb. They are suitable for security for a single building, but are not considered for security lighting of large facilities. This is due to the low illumination they provide.

Quartz   The quartz light provides better illumination and emits a white light. It is activated instantaneously when turned on and has been used to light parking areas. It does have a high energy cost.

Mercury Vapor   The mercury vapor light provides good illumination and emits a white light. It does require a warm-up time and cannot be activated instantaneously. It is used to light parking areas and roadways and has a lower energy cost than the previously mentioned lights.

Sodium Vapor   The sodium vapor light is considered the best for security. It will light instantaneously and has a lower energy cost than all other security lighting. It has excellent penetration at night and in fog due to the amber light. The amber light can distort color on security cameras and upon viewing object by security officer.

Protection of Windows and Utility Ports

All facilities will have windows that will require protection. The first security consideration for window protection is the window itself or what is called glazing, which is the type of glass or plastic used. The more security required, the stronger the glazing should be. The stronger the glazing, the more it will cost. What is used will be based on the threat assessment and whether there are any interior intrusion detection systems being used in the structure.

Window areas can be made of glass, acrylic or what is known as Lexan. The following is a list of the glass, acrylic and Lexan products that can be used for non-bullet resistance protection:

- Annealed glass
- Wire reinforced glass
- Tempered glass
- Laminated glass
- Annealed glass with security film
- Acrylic
- Lexan

Annealed Glass   Annealed glass is also known as windowpane glass. It breaks very easily and provides the least amount of protection of all of the glazing materials. Annealed glass breaks into very sharp shards of glass that can be used as a weapon. These shards can cause injury to individuals in the area if the glazing material is broken by a perpetrator or explosive blast.

Wire Reinforced Glass   Wire reinforced glass is annealed glass with wire imbedded into the glazing. While it looks as if it adds security, it does not and is easily broken. The one advantage is that the glass will not break in large shards because the wire will hold the broken glass together.

Tempered Glass   Tempered glass is a stronger material, but can be defeated easily. When broken, it breaks into small pieces of glass that are relatively harmless. This class was used in older vehicle windscreens.

Laminated Glass   Laminated glass is coated with a plastic. It also can be defeated easily. When broken it holds the glass together in large harmless sheets. This is what is used in vehicle windscreens.

Annealed Glass with Security Film   Annealed glass with security film has a layer of acrylic between two layers of glass. It is difficult to break through this glazing and is the best of the glass products for security protection when bullet resistance is not a requirement.

Acrylic   Acrylic is a plastic and offers little protection. It also breaks into large shards when broken. It also can be scratched easily and will discolor over time due to sunlight.

Lexan   Lexan is a trademark name of a glazing that is impregnable to breakage and is the best of all the security glazing when bullet resistant is not a requirement.

Where bullet resistance is required due to a high threat of robbery or terrorist attack by firearm or explosive devices, the following bullet resistant material can be utilized:

- Bullet resistant glass
- Bullet resistant acrylic
- Lexgard

Bullet Resistant Glass   Bullet resistant glass is a glass glazing that can be from ¼-inch to 1-inch thick. The thicker the glass, the more protection it provides from small arms weapons. It will stop most bullets, but it does cause spalling. Spalling is when the bullet is trapped in the glass. A small particle of glass may break off and fly in the direction away from where the bullet was fired. This can cause injury to anyone near the bullet resistant glass.

Bullet Resistant Acrylic   Bullet resistant acrylic is an acrylic glazing that can be from ¼-inch to 1-inch thick. The thicker the glazing, the more protection it provides from small arms weapons. It will stop most bullets but it does cause spalling.

Figure 6.16   Lexgard bullet resistant glazing shot with a .44 Magnum Smith & Wesson. (Photo by Daniel J. Benny)

Lexgard   Lexgard is the trademark name of an acrylic glazing (see Figure 6.16). The glazing at 1-inch thickness is the best protection from firearms and explosive devices and will stop all small arms weapons and most rifles. With Lexgard, there will be no spalling. This product can be found on the presidential limousines used by the US Secret Service.

Window protection can also be provided by security bars or steel screening. The bars and screens should be securely mounted into the window frame. It is important to make sure that the use of bars and steel screens on the windows does not impede exit in the event of an emergency evacuation.

Utility ports are areas of access into cultural properties for transport of water, air, and trash. These areas can be protected with bars, locks, and intrusion detection systems. Use of security cameras is recommended for trash compactor areas.

Radio Frequency Identification, Magnetometers and X-Ray

Physical security measures can be of value in the protection of property when used at the property's entrance and exit. The concept is to

Figure 6.17 Electromagnetic detection system at the McCormick Library, Harrisburg Area Community College, Harrisburg, PA. (Photo by Daniel J. Benny)

use a security device that is placed on the materials to be protected and to have security detection well as a detection device that is typically located at all exits. The detection devices must be safe for magnetic media and usually have audible and or visible alarms.

There are two primary methods currently used for detection: electromagnetic detection and radio frequency identification (see Figure 6.17).

These technological solutions can prevent, reduce, and detect theft of cultural property collections. Of the two methods, the radio frequency identification is the most effective. The advantage of this system is that it does not require line of sight to be read. The tag combines book or artifact identification and book or artifact security into one label, minimizing labeling time and cost. The tags can be placed on any type of media including CDs, DVDs, and videocassettes. A portion of the RFID memory can be allocated for theft protection so that no other tag is required. Since the anti-theft device is in the label, the security gates do not need to be attached to a central system or interface with the property central database.

Magnetometers   Used at the entrance and exit of the property, a magnetometer, also known as a metal detector, is a physical security device which responds to metal that may not be readily apparent by direct observation. The simplest form of a metal detector consists of an oscillator producing an alternating current that passes through a coil creating an alternating magnetic field. If a piece of electrically conductive metal is close to the coil, eddy currents will be induced in the metal, and this produces an alternating magnetic field of its own. As part of the security system, when another coil is used to measure the magnetic field, acting as a magnetometer, the change in the magnetic field due to the metallic object can be detected.

This can be used to detect the removal of metal objects from the cultural property or from individuals bringing items into the building such as weapons or tools that could be used to defeat a physical security system inside the facility.

X-Ray   The x-ray is used at the entrance and exit of the property to inspect cases, handbags or packages being taken out of or into the property. It is used to detect contraband, weapons, explosives entering the facility or artifacts, and collections being removed. The use of an x-ray in most cases will deter such activity and can, of course, detect such attempts.

Bibliography

Baker, P. & Benny, D. J. (2012) *Complete Guide to Physical Security.* Boca Raton, FL: CRC Press.
Fischer, R. J. & Green, G. (2004). *Introduction to Security* (7th ed.). Burlington, MA: Elsevier.
Mason, D.L. (1979) *The Fine Art of Art Security.* New York, NY: Van Nostrand Reinhold Company.

7

SECURITY DEPARTMENT

Chief Security Officer

When establishing a security department, the hiring of a security professional as head or chief security officer (CSO) is the first priority. The selection of this individual is critical to the success of the operation of the security department. The individual selected should have at minimum a bachelor's degree from an accredited university or college in security administration or criminal justice with a master's degree or doctorate preferred. The CSO should report to the CEO.

A security professional with professional security certification should also be considered. There are two security-related certifications that would be of value to the CSO. The first is offered by the American Society for Industrial Security International (ASIS International). ASIS International has developed a professional security certification, the Certified Protection Professional (CPP) that is accepted both nationally and internationally by the security profession as well as the US Department of Homeland Security and the Transportation Security Administration.

The CPP has been established for individuals working in security supervision and management. The CPP designation is bestowed when the candidate has successfully completed the comprehensive examination which covers all aspects of the security management profession including management methods, security force management, legal issues, investigations, physical security, protective service, terrorism, and budgeting.

A professional security certification directly related to counterespionage is the Certified Confidentiality Officer (CCO). The CCO designation is offered by the Business Espionage Control and Countermeasures Association to candidates who have successfully completed the comprehensive examination covering all aspects of counterespionage

Determining the Size of the Security Department

Once the CSO is hired, that individual must work with the CEO to determine the size of the security department required. The size of the security department will be based on several factors. These factors include a physical security survey of the property to be protected. The duties and functions of the security department must be based on the security threat.

The physical security survey and the physical security measures to be utilized at the cultural property will have an impact on the number of security officers required to provide adequate protection.

The use of intrusion detection systems, security cameras, security lights, fire protections systems and access control such as proximity card readers may reduce the number of security officers required to patrol the property. If there are no or limited physical security measures, it will be necessary to establish a larger security force in order to effectively secure the site. The use of more physical security measures may allow for the reduction of the size of the force. Regardless of the level of physical security protection, in most cases there will be a need for security officers to monitor the intrusion, fire, access control, and camera systems. Security officers must also be able to respond to the various alarms or activity observed on security cameras.

For each security post to be covered twenty-four hours a day, the organization will need to hire four security officers to account for days off, holidays, and vacations. So, if two security officers are required to be on duty twenty-four hours, eight security officers will need to be hired.

Mission of the Security Department

In establishing the size of the security force, the mission and duties of the security department must be determined. The primary duty of a security force is to provide proactive patrols of the property in order to protect life, prevent losses, respond to emergencies, and to provide assistance to staff and visitors.

Security patrols may be conducted by foot within the buildings. Outdoors and in parking areas, automobiles, all wheel drive vehicles, bicycles, or segways, may be used.

The security department may also be utilized to control access to the property. Access control may begin at the perimeter of the property and at vehicle entrances. If so, the security department will be responsible for verifying the identity of drivers and, if necessary, may also conduct inspections of vehicles entering the property. Access control points covered by security officers may also include entrances. Additionally, the security department is often charged with escorting visitors in restricted areas. Security officers may also be assigned to transport money, high value property, or company confidential information. These assignments may take place on the property or off in the case of escorting money to a banking facility. Providing escorts to employee parking areas for employees leaving work during hours of darkness may also be a service provided by the security department.

Depending on the size of the property and the number of buildings, inspections of the facility for security threats, safety and loss hazards are functions that should be performed by the security officers while on patrol.

Investigations of losses, safety issues, accidents, violations of regulations and employee misconduct, and counterespionage will require the attention of investigators if there is a significant case load based on the size and population of the facility. In most cases, this function is conducted by the CSO.

Monitoring of intrusion detection and fire safety systems, security cameras, and access control points is an import function of security. The establishment of a proprietary security communications and monitoring center to dispatch security staff, answer security related calls, monitor the security, fire safety, cameras, and access control points will require hiring additional security officers. These positions should be staffed by trained security officers who can be rotated between patrol functions and monitoring duties. This is critical since a trained security officer will be more effective at responding to security calls and situations arising while monitoring the security and safety systems than a person hired only to work in the communications center. It is also important to not have an individual monitor such systems for more than two hours. A security officer will become less effective at monitoring a security camera if the assignment lasts more than two hours. Security officers working in the communications center can be rotated to the patrol function after two hours in the communications center.

The final function to consider is the administrative duties associated with a security department. These duties include securing security department records, processing of internal violations such as parking tickets, and preparing correspondence, monthly reports along with any other administrative duties that may be required. These positions may be in the role of secretary to the director or administrative clerks.

A final determination of what services and duties the security department will perform needs to be made based on a review of all the possible duties and functions of a security department that have been described.

Legal Authorization to Protect the Facility

The administrators and the CSO must know the state laws relating to apprehension of suspects. They should review their state's laws before making any citizen's arrest for espionage, theft, or any other criminal offense.

Security officers are authorized to enforce all property rules and regulations pertaining to security, safety, fire protection, parking, traffic, and vehicle registration at the facility. This enforcement is accomplished through the writing of reports and verbal directions or commands as the situation warrants.

Security officers have the authority to stop anyone on the organization's property where they are employed for the purpose of identifying such persons or determining if they are authorized to be in a specific area. Officers may also stop anyone to investigate a suspicious activity or to obtain information regarding an individual who they believe has committed a criminal offense.

An arrest is the taking of a person into custody in order that he or she may be held to answer for or be prevented from committing a criminal offense. Citizen's arrests in most states can only be made for felonies committed in the presence of the security officer and for the safety and protection of life.

The criminal code and other laws relating to the authority of security officers of the state in which the facility is located must be consulted. Each security officer should be responsible for knowing and understanding the state laws and must be trained in this area.

Pedestrian Stops

With probable cause, security officers should be authorized to stop anyone on the facility property to ascertain his or her identity and that person's purpose for being at the facility or in a specific area of the facility. Probable cause includes individuals acting in a suspicious manner, loitering, being in unauthorized areas or during periods when the facility is closed to the public.

All staff members should be required to carry a photo identification card while on duty and should be required show it upon request. Should a staff member, refuse to show identification, an incident report should be filed.

Should a person be stopped and refuse to show identification, that person should be escorted off of the property. Any pedestrian stop should be documented in the security officer's daily activity report. Should the stop be the result of a significant incident, an incident report should be completed.

Profile and Security Threat

A review of the profile of the facility to be protected is necessary when determining the size of the security department. The type of facility with regard to its size, hours of operation, number of employees, and visitors as well as security threats are the key elements that must be considered in making a determination concerning the size of the security department.

The security threat will be based on numerous factors including the type of property type and the type of protected information at the location. The local crime rate and previous crime and losses against the facility must also be evaluated to determine the current risk to people, and property.

Size of the Facility

The size of the facility including the square footage of buildings, the number of floors in the buildings, the total number of protected documents and media stored in the facility must be calculated in determining the number of security officers required to provide adequate protection.

Hours of Operation

Hours of operations will impact the size of the security department. If a facility is open during normal office hours, a detection system can be used at night. This will obviously require smaller security force coverage than a period of longer operations. As hours of operation lessen or expand based on the specific situation, the level of security coverage will also need to be adjusted.

Number of Employees and Visitors

The number of employees will also have an impact on the size of the security department. The numbers may change according to the day of the week and hours of the day and this fluctuation will need to be calculated into the facility's security coverage.

Proprietary Security Force

A proprietary security force is one in which the security officers are employees of the facility. A proprietary security force may be full-time, part-time or a combination. Based on the type of position, security officers may qualify for full or limited company benefits such as medical coverage, insurance, vacation, and sick leave.

The advantages of a proprietary security force include having control over who is hired by establishing standards and qualifications for the positions and the conducting of an extensive pre-employment background investigation. With a proprietary security force, there is more opportunity to provide professional and effective staff training. In addition, a proprietary security force will have more loyalty to the organization because the officers are employees and because of the benefit and training packages offered. This leads to a reduction in turnover. Long-term security officers will be an asset to the organization because of their experience.

The disadvantages of a proprietary security force are that it takes longer to hire staff and costs more as the facility must place advertisements for recruitment, conduct pre-employment background investigations and supply uniforms and equipment. There is also the cost of a complete benefits package.

Another disadvantage is that once the security officer makes it past the probationary period, termination is more difficult. To do so, all actions must be documented and progressive disciplinary action must be utilized unless the offenses are serious enough to warrant immediate termination.

Contract Security Force

A contract security force is composed of security officers working as employees of a licensed security or investigative firm that provides security service on a contractual basis. These officers are not on the firm's payroll. In most states, contract security providers must be licensed, so it is important to select a firm that meets this legal requirement.

The advantage of utilizing a contract security force is that there is the flexibility to hire full- or part-time or a combination of both for whatever length of time required. The company utilizing contract security does not need to place ads to recruit, interview, or hire the officers. It is less expensive because the licensed contractor pays for the benefits, training, equipment, and uniforms of the security officers. Another advantage is that contract security officers are easy to terminate. If an officer is not performing well, the security contractor can remove the officer from the property and replace him or her with another security officer.

Disadvantages include a lack of loyalty on the part of the contract security officers to firm that they are assigned; their loyalty in most cases will be with the licensed agency. The training provided by the contracting agency may not be at the level of a proprietary security force. There may also be a high turnover rate due to the lower pay received by contract security officers or officers may be pulled from one work location to another by the contract security firm to meet various client schedule demands.

There are advantages and disadvantages to both proprietary and contract security. The company needs to make a determination as to which best fulfills its requirements and budget. The organization can utilize full-time proprietary security officers, full-time contractor security officers or a combination of both.

Security Department Uniforms and Identification

Traditionally security officers wear uniforms. A uniform is a symbol of authority and allows the security officer to be easily identified during an emergency or when assistance is required by staff or visitors. The most common security uniform is slacks and a short or long sleeve police/military style shirt with a security patch, name tag, and a badge where authorized by state or local laws.

During colder weather, a variety of light and heavy weight water resistant jackets and coats can be utilized. Patches, name tags and badges are also placed on the outer garment for ease of identification. Headgear is also part of the security uniform and can be a more formal eight-point cap, trooper hat or ball cap style with a badge or security insignia placed on the front of the headwear.

A softer uniform image is may be selected rather than the traditional security uniform. This often consists of a jacket, shirt, tie, and slacks that may have a security patch attached with a name tag. Where permitted by law, a security badge may be displayed on the jacket using a pocket holder. In warmer season or climates, the softer uniform may be slacks with a shirt and tie or a polo type shirt with security patches, name tag and badge. The security attire may be business dress or business casual rather than a distinctive uniform. If this type of clothing is utilized, a name tag and security badge in a pocket holder should be utilized for easy identification as a security officer.

Just as the security uniform provides a symbol, so does security department identification. Badges, where authorized by state and local law, are universally recognized symbols of authority. Shoulder patches also add to the authority of the security officer and identify the company or contract agency by which they are employed. The most important aspect of security identification is a photo identification card to be worn on the uniform or carried in a case. This will provide for positive identification of the security officer where he or she works.

Security uniforms and identification allow the security officer to be identified as an authority figure, but the authority also comes from legal codes that apply to the security officer depending on the state in which he or she operates. The authority is also derived from the organization by which the security officer is employed. This legitimacy must also be based on the proper use of such authority.

Staff and Visitor Identification

Every staff member should be issued a photo identification card and it should be worn in plain view at work. This allows for immediate identification of authorized individuals in restricted areas of the property that are not open to the public. The wearing of the photo identification by staff also permits visitors to identify staff members if they need assistance or have questions. The photo identification cards should also be utilized for access control. When using proximity card readers on property doors, the photo identification cards can also be proximity cards utilized to operate the access control units on the doors. The same card can also be used for timekeeping.

The wearing of photo identification by staff can also be of value in the prevention of crime. As staff members walk about the property, they will be identified by potential perpetrators and that could deter criminal activity.

Visitor identification should be utilized for visitors who will be accessing restricted areas not open to the public. This will allow staff and security to identify authorized visitors to these areas and provide documentation of the visitor arrival and departure as the visitor identification is signed out to the visitor and then returned by the visitor.

The computer-based photo identification system, card access system, and visitor identification should be administered by the security department. Strict inventory control must be established on all staff and visitor identification issued.

Security Department Protective Equipment

Where authorized by law, protective equipment may be considered for the security department. The type of protective equipment utilized will be based on the threat level, location and the mission of the security department and may range from handcuffs to carrying firearms. Many states require specialized training before officers are authorized to carry various type of protective equipment. In Pennsylvania, for example, security officers who carry a baton or firearm must complete what is known as the Lethal Weapons Act 235 Course. To attend the forty-hour course the student must submit to a criminal background check and medical and psychological evaluations. The forty-hour course covers the legal aspects of carrying a weapon, the authority of a security officer, the use of force considerations and the Pennsylvania Crimes Code. Students must pass a written test and qualify on the firing range to become certified under the Lethal Weapons Act. It is important to know the requirements with regard to carrying a weapon in the state in which the security officers are operating to ensure compliance with that state's laws.

Handcuffs

Handcuffs are important should the security officer be required to make a citizen's arrest in the performance of his or her duties. Handcuffs provide a means of securing an individual who becomes violent either before or after a citizen's arrest. The use of handcuffs in such situations provides for the safety of the security officer and the public. The handcuffs should be of good quality and have the capability of being doubled locked. The double-locking mechanism prevents the handcuff from being tightened by accident and avoids the possibility that the suspect will claim an injury from their use.

Oleoresin Capsicum Spray

Oleoresin capsicum or OC spray is a lachrymatory irritant agent that can be carried by security officers. It provides a nonlethal method of self defense for the security officer and is very effective in most situations. Security officers should be certified by the manufacturer of the oleoresin capsicum product to ensure proper use and to avoid liability issues.

Batons

Batons have been carried by security for more than a hundred years and they can be used as both defensive and offensive protective tools. When used offensively, they are considered deadly weapons. Batons come in various styles including the traditional striate baton, the collapsible ASP baton, and the PR-24 full size or collapsible model (see Figure 7.1). Certification should be obtained from the manufacturer of the particular baton that is carried for proper use and liability protection.

Firearms

Firearms may be carried by the security department based on the legal requirements and regulations of the state. The threat and mission of the security department at a particular site must also be considered. It is the view of the author that institutional protection officers should be armed if authorized by law. If security officers carry firearms, they

Figure 7.1   PR-24 Baton and ASP Baton. (Photo by Daniel J. Benny)

Figure 7.2   A Walther P-38 9mm, Walther PPK.32l, Beretta 92F 9mm, and Beretta.25l are examples of semiautomatic pistols used in security over the years. (Photo by Daniel J. Benny)

must be equipped with an alternate means of protective equipment such as a baton and oleoresin capsicum. This gives the security officer a non-lethal response option if use of deadly force would not be authorized based on the situation.

A revolver or semi-automatic firearm may be carried (see Figures 7.2 and 7.3). In some situations, security officers may also carry shotguns when transporting a cultural property of high value by vehicle. In addition to state legal requirements for qualification and certification, security officers should be trained and qualified at least once a year with the weapons and ammunition they carry. Many security departments require such training and qualification twice and as many as four times a year.

Security officers who carry this protective equipment must be trained in the use of force continuum and the company use of force policy.

Use of Force Continuum

- Security officer presence — No force is used. Considered the best way to resolve a situation.

Figure 7.3 The Smith & Wesson .357. Magnum and the Colt 38 Detective Special are examples of revolvers that have been used by security over the years. (Photo by Daniel J. Benny)

- The mere presence of a security officer works to deter crime or diffuse a situation.
- Security officers' attitudes are professional and nonthreatening.
- Verbalization — Force is not-physical.
  - Security officers issue calm, nonthreatening commands, such as "Let me see your identification."
  - Security officers may increase their volume and shorten commands in an attempt to gain compliance. Short commands might include "Stop," or "Don't move."
- Empty-hand control — Security officers use bodily force to gain control of a situation.
  - *Soft technique.* Security officers use grabs, holds and joint locks to restrain an individual.
  - *Hard technique.* Security officers use punches and kicks to restrain an individual.
- Less lethal methods — Security officers use less-lethal technologies to gain control of a situation.
  - *Blunt impact.* Security officers may use a baton to immobilize a combative person.

- *Chemical.* Security officers may use chemical sprays or projectiles embedded with chemicals to restrain an individual.
- Lethal force — Security officers use lethal weapons to gain control of a situation. Should only be used if a suspect poses a serious threat to the security officer or another individual.
- Security officers use deadly weapons such as firearms or baton striking vital area of the body (head, neck, kidney or groin) to stop an individual's actions.

Security Department Vehicles

The security department may maintain and operate patrol vehicles for use at the property for the patrol of parking areas and roadways. Based on the size of the property and climate conditions, an automobile may be used or a four-wheel drive vehicle may be selected.

The vehicles should be visibly marked as security vehicles of the property. Security/emergency lighting and sound producing devices should be utilized if permitted in accordance with state law (see Figure 7.4). The vehicles should also be equipped with a public address system, police scanner, and radio.

Other types of patrol modes may be utilized. If the company is located on a water way there may be maritime security patrols using a watercraft (see Figure 7.5).

Lighting

Emergency lighting, where permitted by state law, should be utilized when stopping on roadways or parking areas during vehicle inquiries. Emergency lighting may also be used when responding to calls on the property, when conducting traffic control, or for increased visibility during routine patrol.

Security Department Communications

Several means of communication should be available to the security department to ensure immediate and effective communication

Figure 7.4 Security patrol vehicle at Harrisburg Area Community College, Harrisburg, PA. (Photo by Daniel J. Benny)

Figure 7.5 The author's Boston Whaler, a US Coast Guard Auxiliary Facility patrol boat, in the Susquehanna River near Three Mile Island, Middletown, PA. (Photo by Daniel J. Benny)

Figure 7.6 Security force communications, telephone, mobile phone and security radios. (Photo by Daniel J. Benny)

during both routine and emergency situations. These should include portable two-way radios and mobile two-way radios if there are security vehicles on the property (see Figure 7.6). Emergency call boxes are recommended throughout the property including inside the building, outside parking and walkway areas to be used by security, staff or visitors if there is an emergency. The use of mobile telephones by security officers is also recommended for emergency communications. A method to make public announcement is recommended in the event of an emergency such as dealing with an active shooter on the property and also to aid in evacuations.

When using any form of communication, members of the security department must be expected to communicate in a professional and service-oriented manner. When using two-way radios, FCC guidelines must be followed. At no time while talking on any type of communications equipment should members of the security department utilize CB or other types of slang or jargon, nor will profanity be used on the communication system.

Security Department Reports

In order to document incidents, complaints and activities in which the security department becomes involved, various reports will be required. All reports should be entered on a computer, if possible. Typewritten or reports printed in ink using block letters are acceptable.

Completed security department reports are to be considered legal documents because they may be utilized in criminal, civil, governmental or other proceedings. Reports and the information contained in them must be protected.

Incident/Complaint Report and Continuation Report

The incident/complaint report form should be utilized to document any complaints received and all important incidents which occur on the property. The type of incidents to be reported include criminal activity, accidents, vehicle accidents, medical emergencies, fire or safety emergencies, hazmat spills, reports of suspicious activity, and any other incident or activity in which any member of the security department becomes involved or believes is worth documenting. If in doubt, the security officer should complete an incident/complaint report.

Each incident/complaint report should be numbered beginning with the year, the month, and numerical report number for the calendar year. For example, January 12, 2013, the date of the first report of the year, would read as 01-12-2013-001. January 13, 2013 the date of the second report would read; 01-13-2013-002.

Daily Activity Report

All security officers should complete a daily activity report during their shift. This report will be utilized to document their times of arrival and departure, inspections of the patrol vehicle, where applicable, and to document routine activities. Routine activities include building and door unlocking and locking, escorts, and checks of buildings in various areas of the cultural property. The daily activity report should also show the initial response to an incident or complaint and reference the incident/complaint report number. The daily activity report should be maintained on file in the security office.

The security department training records for all security staff members need to be maintained by the CSO and used to document each individual officer's training.

Protection of Security Department Information

All information, whether received orally or in written form, pertaining to security department incidents or investigations being conducted is confidential information. Such information should only be disseminated to authorized individuals with a need to know. Information should not be released to individuals not associated with the cultural property unless approved by the CSO. Any requests for information from members of the media should be referred to the CSO.

All sensitive security documents must be secured in a locked security container when not being used. This includes both final and draft copies of incident reports, statements, investigative notes, safety and security reports, audits and inspections. Sensitive documents which are no longer needed will be shredded prior to placing them in removal containers.

Ethics and Conduct

Ethics

All security department personnel are expected to maintain the highest professional and moral standards. The quality of a professional security department ultimately depends upon the willingness of its staff to observe special standards of conduct and to manifest good faith in professional relationships.

The following Professional Code of Ethics, as established by the American Society for Industrial Security International, will distinguish the professional from the non-professionals.

AMERICAN SOCIETY FOR INDUSTRIAL SECURITY INTERNATIONAL PROFESSIONAL CODE OF ETHICS

I. Perform professional duties in accordance with the laws and highest moral principles.

II. Observe the precepts of truthfulness, honesty, and integrity.

III. Be faithful and diligent in discharging professional responsibilities.

IV. Be competent in discharging professional responsibilities.

V. Do not maliciously injure the professional reputation of colleagues.

Security Department Training

One of the most important aspects of the management of a security department is to ensure that the security officers are effectively trained to meet any state regulations as well as security industry standards of training. Such training will promote professionalism and reduce the liability risk. Security force training can be accomplished by on-the-job experience and training and through the use of various formal education methods.

On-the-job experience and training involve of a structured and documented approach in instructing new security officers with regard to their day-to-day duties. Each new security officer should be assigned to a mentor. The mentor may be a supervisor, lead officer or training officer who will guide the new officer through his or her daily activities, providing instruction on how to perform assigned duties. As each new task is learned, it should be documented in a written training record and placed in the new security officer's file.

As security officers accumulate time in the profession and participate in various security assignments, they will gain knowledge and proficiency. Other on-the-job educational tools may include having security officers take part in organizational meetings and committees to expand their professional knowledge. This may also include being part of the security and safety committee or attending meetings related to special events that might be scheduled.

In addition to on-the-job training, formal educational methods should also be applied. These may include company assistance that enables the security officer to obtain a college degree in security or criminal justice. In-service training can also be used, where the security officer is provided with information in a classroom environment covering security procedures, report writing, patrol methods or court testimony. In-service training can also be used to provide the security officer with various certifications such as first aid and CPR, handcuff, OC or baton certification.

Another option for education is to have the security officer take part in self-study by online proprietary training or a website offering free training such as the Homeland Security Federal Emergency Management Agency Academy. Time for such online training can be provided during the work schedule or it can be accomplished off duty. Directed reading is another source of education where articles or documents related to security are made available in the security office. Security officers would be required to read and sign off on the documents that they have read.

In order to ensure that the security department is professionally trained, a security training program needs to be established and mandatory training needs to be provided to all security officers. All state regulatory training requirements, where applicable, must be completed. It is important that all training completed by each security officer be documented in the officer's training file. This will allow for the tracking of the training to ensure that it has been completed and provide such documentation as may be required by regulatory agencies or related to liability issues.

Professional Security Certifications

Professional security certification can be obtained and is of value to those in the security profession. As previously discussed, the American Society for Industrial Security (ASIS International) has developed several professional security certifications for individuals working in security supervision and management. ASIS also offers two certifications for non-management security professionals. The Professional

Certified Investigator (PCI) was established for security investigators or private investigators. The designation of PCI is bestowed upon successful completion of the examination that covers all aspect of security and private investigation including investigative methods, legal considerations, and interview methods.

The Physical Security Professional (PSP) designation is designed for those in security who are responsible for physical security within an institutional property such as a museum, historic site, archive or library. The examination covers intrusion detection systems, barriers, security cameras, and lock and access control. Upon successful completion of the examination, the designation of PSP is bestowed.

As previously discussed the Certified Confidential Officer (CCO) designation bestowed by the Business Espionage Controls and Countermeasures Association may also be considered for security supervisors and officers. It would be of value in the protection of company confidential and US classified information.

Security Patrols

The primary duty of a security officer is to patrol the property. The purpose of the patrol function is to have the security officer at the right place at the right time to prevent losses due to criminal activity, safety concerns, and during an emergency. A uniformed security officer also provides a deterrent as a symbol of authority as he or she patrols the property.

Foot patrol is the most common method of security patrol inside of a structure. It allows for close observation of the property and positive interaction with the cultural property staff and visitors. In large structures, small battery operated security vehicles may be deployed for fast response, especially if there is a need to transport emergency equipment or individuals. Foot patrol is also utilized to patrol walkways, parking areas, and other exterior segments of the property.

Properties with expansive parking areas, roadways, and open areas cannot be patrolled effectively by security officers on foot, especially during periods of cold and inclement weather. In these situations, the security officer must be able to cover large areas in a timely manner during both routine patrol and in response to service calls and emergencies.

The most common means of patrol in this situation is a motor vehicle assigned to the security department. It should be clearly marked as a security vehicle. It may be an automobile or an all wheel drive vehicle. The vehicle chosen should be determined by the types of roadways and layout of the property as well as the climate. Security management of a property located in an area that receives snowfall should consider the use of an all wheel drive security vehicle to ensure that security patrols can be accomplished in inclement weather or where off road capabilities are needed.

During warm weather, bicycles may be considered as patrol vehicles. They allow fast response and are a valuable public relations tool because they promote more interaction between staff and visitors to the property.

All security patrols must be conducted in a random manner so that patterns and predictability cannot be established. If the security patrol becomes predictable, then individuals intent on taking part in criminal activities including industrial espionage can plan their activities without fear of being discovered by security patrols. If patrol patterns are established, the security officers can become complacent and less observant of their surroundings, thus reducing their effectiveness.

To reduce predictability, the security officer on patrol should use the concept of back tracking. For example, the officer would make a security walk through an area then turn around and walk back through the same area or walking up a flight of stairs, turning around and walking back down again.

The two categories of patrol are supervised and unsupervised. Supervised patrol is one that is monitored and tracked by the use of proximity readers placed throughout the museum, historic site, archive or library structures and grounds that the security officer must activate as he or she makes the set number of security rounds during the patrol schedule. This can also be accomplished by having the security officer communicate with the property's central station at set points during the patrol route.

The goal of this method is to document that the security patrol did, in fact, cover all areas of the property and, if monitored live, to be alerted if the security office does not scan the reader. This provides safety for the officer in the event that there is a security incident taking place or in case the officer has an accident or medical emergency. This method of supervised patrol is recommended when the security officer is conducting patrol during times when the property is closed or when patrolling remote areas of the property.

During hours when the property is open to the public, supervised patrol is not recommended. During these periods, the security officer does not need to check in at specified points on a patrol route. For the officer's safety, he or she should be required to check in by radio at predetermined times during a patrol schedule. The reason a supervised method of patrol is not recommended when the cultural property is open is that the security office will be more concerned in documenting the supervised patrol and, as a result, may not be as effective in interacting with visitors and staff.

The awareness color code can be used to illustrate the proper attentiveness of a security officer during the course of their assigned shift.

White: This is when the security officer is unaware of his or her surroundings. The security officer is thinking of personal matters rather than being alert during patrol. A security officer on patrol in the white awareness mode is not doing the job and is placing the officer, the visitors and the staff at risk.

Green: This is the awareness color code for normal patrol. A security officer can and should be at this level of awareness during the entire patrol. In fact, it is the level that everyone should be at when out and about in public places. At this level, security officers will use all of their senses. Vision is the number one sensor wherein the security officer can see all potential and actual threats. Hearing is the second most important sense. A security officer may hear an alarm going off, a call for help, or a transmission on the security radio. The officer may also hear someone approaching in low visibility. Smell is also an important sensor. A security officer may smell smoke or a natural gas leak and be able to prevent a serious incident. If a suspicious person approaches the security officer and the person approaching security is intoxicated or has been smoking marijuana, the officer may be able to smell it and be alert to an individual who may not be in his or her normal state of mind. The final sense is touch. This may be of value to the security officer in determining if equipment is overheating or if a vehicle found on the property parking areas was recently driven as indicated by the engine heat on the hood of the vehicle.

Yellow: This is the level when the security officer is alert to something unusual based on one of the officer's senses. The security officer becomes alert and begins to evaluate the situation and to make a determination if it needs further investigation or if he or she should return to normal patrol awareness or the green mode.

Red: This is the full reaction mode wherein the security officer must respond to protect himself or herself, others or the facility. If the security officer is alert he or she should never be surprised and go from the green to the red mode. With that said, no one is perfect and it can happen.

It is critical that the security officers know their patrol area. This means that they should have a working knowledge of the physical layout of the site including the interior of all buildings and the exterior property. The security officers need to know what is normal based on the time of day and day of the week. This alerts them to suspicious criminal activity or safety hazards. Security officers should also be aware of any special activities occurring during their patrol schedule such as special events, construction or an area of the property that may be temporarily closed to the public.

When conducting patrols, security officers should utilize the concepts of loss prevention and assets protection with the goal of preventing losses due to criminal activities and safety hazards. Patrols should be highly visible so that visitors and staff members see uniformed security officers frequently. This means that any potential criminal, spy or terrorist will also see security officers and their presence may deter unwanted activity.

Apprehension and Arrest

Members of the security department are not police officers and generally will not make apprehensions and arrests. They should only act in accordance with state laws and company policies. Apprehensions and arrests may only be conducted in instances where the security officer witnesses the commission of a felony. Security officers may also make an apprehension of a violent person in order to protect themselves or another person from bodily harm.

Bibliography

Fischer, R. J. and Green, G. (2004). *Introduction to Security* (7th ed.). Burlington, MA: Elsevier.

Kovacich, G.L and Halibozek, E.P. (2004). *The Manager's Handbook for Corporate Security*, Burlington, MA: Elsevier.

8

THE HUMAN RESOURCES DEPARTMENT AND COUNTERESPIONAGE

The human resources department plays an important role in the prevention of industrial espionage. One of the best methods of counterespionage is to utilize the human resources department to establish position descriptions, work policies and conduct an effective screening process to reduce the risk of industrial espionage from internal threats.

Position Description and Separation of Functions

The HR role begins with the writing of the position description that clarifies each employee's duties. As part of the position description, it will set forth which positions in the organization will have access to company-protected information.

The development of position descriptions is vital in the advertising, hiring, and even promotion of individuals in the work place. It is not only a legal requirement to comply with state regulations and federal laws such as the American with Disabilities Act. It is important to clarify each employee's duties based on his or her position in the organization.

If the organization is working on US projects dealing with classified information, the job description as related to counterespionage should detail what company-protected or US classified information the employee will have access to in the course of his or her duties. This is establishing the "need to know," which is a requirement before any employee should be able to access protected information. Access to protected information should not be given in a cavalier manner, but only when employees actually need access to such information to perform the duties of their positions as described in the position description.

When developing the position descriptions wherein employees will have access to company-protected information, the duties of the various employees should be divided into separate functions that should be identified in the position description. Separation of functions means that one person should not be in a position based on his or her job description to have total access to any process dealing with company-protected information. This is to prevent one individual from being able to access and manipulate the procedures in place that protect company-protected or US classified information. The goal is to require numerous positions and oversight of such processes. This is an important preventive measure as part of the total counter espionage plan.

Pre-Employment Background Investigation

The human resources department, often in conjunction with the security department, conducts initial screenings and background investigations of all new job applicants. This investigatory process can be used to eliminate an applicant who may be pre-disposed to theft and/or industrial espionage. A professional pre-employment background investigation may determine if an individual is a possible industrial espionage future threat based on loyalty, lifestyle, or other issues that could lead to blackmail or a need for money attained through espionage. A complete background investigation may expose an applicant who is attempting to obtain a position with the organization solely for the purpose of conducting industrial espionage.

The depth of the background investigation will depend on the applicant, his or her potential position in the organization, that position's functions, and threat level. All of the following areas need to be examined for a full scope background investigation. In some cases, only some of the areas will be checked or perhaps all areas but not in as much detail.

Applicants need to complete written application forms in their own handwriting and the forms need to be signed and dated. Even if a resume was accepted online, at some point the written application needs to be completed. This will give the organization justification for not hiring the applicant or for termination should false statements be discovered before or after hiring the applicant.

The areas that need to be investigated as part of the pre-employment inquiry will include the following:

- Criminal records
- Civil records
- Driving records
- Employment history
- Professional licenses and certifications
- Education
- Memberships
- Financial history
- Military service
- Personal and professional references
- Residence inquiry
- Family
- Lifestyle
- Medical
- Internet search

Criminal Records

A review of the applicant's criminal record is critical. Depending on the jurisdiction in which the business is located, most county court houses and state governments allow a search of the criminal record. In some areas, this can be completed through the agency holding the records web site. In other situations, a criminal history record may need to be done in person at the local or state jurisdiction.

Private business will not be able to conduct national criminal record checks. The only exception is if the organization is working with US classified information as a contractor for the government. Even then, the company will not have access to a national criminal database, but the government investigating agency will.

Another area to search is the national sexual offender list. An individual on a list of sexual offenders and working for a company is vulnerable to being blackmailed into conducting industrial espionage. These lists are also available on a state-by-state level. These lists are coordinated by the Department of Justice and enable every citizen to search the latest information from all 50 states, the District of Columbia, Puerto Rico, Guam, and numerous Native American tribes. It also provides links so one can also search registry websites maintained by individual jurisdictions.

Civil Records

Civil records can be searched for records of divorce, marriage, or any civil action by or against the applicant. Special attention should be given to civil suits filed against the applicant or any civil actions filed by the applicant against previous employers. This is especially important if any of the civil actions against the individual were for the disclosure of company information or violation of any non-disclosure or non-competitive agreements.

Civil records can also identify any property that an individual may own. This property could be home, rental property, or commercial business property. The property could also be acreage with no structure on the land.

Driving Records

When reviewing an applicant's driving record obtained from the state's department of motor vehicles, make note of the type of car the applicant owns, determine if it fits with the applicant's current income level. Other areas to be checked include any records of accidents, violations, suspensions, or revocations of the applicant's driving license. The driving records must also be checked for serious violations such as driving under the influence or any death by motor vehicle.

Employment History

A review of the applicant's employment history should include all positions the applicant has held for at least the past ten years. The details should include the title of the position, salary, duties, awards and achievements, the supervisor's name and the reason for leaving.

Red flags include gaps in time, moving for a higher level position and higher pay position to a position at a lower level and less pay.

Periods of unemployment should be examined to determine why the applicant was unemployed.

If possible, go to the employers in person. If that is not possible, make contact by phone rather than by mail or email in an attempt to verify the applicant's employment and performance.

Professional Licenses and Certifications

If the position the applicant is applying for requires a professional license or certification then such license and certification requirements must be verified. If there is no requirement for a special license or certification but the applicant lists them on the application, they should be verified. Many applicants list list items on their applications to embellish their profiles thinking that the items listed will not be investigated. If the person's list of licenses or certifications are not true—even if not required, then this obliviously indicates that the person is dishonest and could be one who takes part in industrial espionage if the opportunity avails itself.

Licenses may vary from a state commercial driver's license, a pilot's license issued by the Federal Aviation Administration, a boat captain's license from the US Coast Guard, a medical license or even a state private investigator's license.

Certifications may include teaching certifications from a state agency. Others may be industry certifications such as Certified Protection Professional, (CPP) from ASIS International, Certified Safety Professional (CSP) from the American Society of Safety Engineers, or Certified Confidentially Officer (CCO) from the Business Espionage Controls and Countermeasure Association.

Education

Educational credentials are important, especially if there are educational requirements for the position. The types of educational credential may include:

- High school diploma
- Trade school
- Two-year college
- Four-year university

- Graduate university

When documenting education at the high school or trade school level, a diploma will confirm it, but if unavailable, a call to the school for verification will also confirm it. For college and university degrees, a copy of the diploma may be accepted, but official school transcripts sent directly from the college or university to the employer are important. Ensure that the college or university is licensed by the state in which it is located. A reputable college or university will be accredited by one of the regional accrediting agencies in the United States as follows:

The Higher Learning Commission of the North Central
  Association of Colleges and Schools
30 North LaSalle, Suite 2400, Chicago, IL 60602

Middle States Commission on Higher Education
3624 Market Street, Philadelphia, PA 19104

New England Association of Schools and Colleges
Commission on Institutions of Higher Education
209 Burlington Road, Bedford, MA 01730-1433

Northwest Commission on Colleges and Universities
8060 165th Avenue, NW, Suite 100, Redmond, WA 98052
(425) 558-4224

Southern Association of Schools and Colleges
Commission on Colleges
1866 Southern Lane, Decatur, GA 30033-4097
(404) 679-4500

Western Association of Schools and Colleges
Accrediting Commission for Senior Colleges and Universities
985 Atlantic Avenue, Suite 100, Alameda, CA 94501
(510) 748-9001

Western Association of Schools and Colleges
Accrediting Commission for Community and Junior Colleges
10 Commercial Blvd., Suite 204, Novato, CA 94949
(415) 506-0234

Diplomas or degrees from unaccredited or unlicensed colleges and universities should not be accepted as meeting the applicant's educational requirements. Be aware of educational credentials from diploma mills. These are schools that are unlicensed and or unaccredited and will issue degrees with no work for a fee.

Memberships

Memberships listed by the applicant should be looked at very closely because they can tell a great deal about an individual's interests and lifestyle. Memberships may include professional organizations related to the work they do. Organizations may also include community or social groups. It is not permissible to ask about political or religious organizations, but membership in any recognized subversive group is an issue of concern.

Financial History

The applicant's financial history is important in that it reveals his or her financial situation and any possible indebtedness and assets. Since the primary motive for industrial espionage is money, knowing the applicant's financial situation is critical in determining if there could be a threat from espionage. This includes authorizing a credit report and checking other financial references.

Military Service

When checking the applicant's military service, the information to be reviewed includes the branch of service—the Navy, Army, Air Force Marines, Coast Guard or Merchant Marine. In addition, the applicant's dates of service, duty assignments, military training, awards and any disciplinary actions must be reviewed as part of the process.

The discharge should be honorable. A discharge for any other reason should be investigated to determine the reason of the separation. A review of the DD-214 and DD256N forms issued by the military will confirm the type of discharge.

A search of military records can be done through the National Personnel Records Center, Military Personnel Records (NPRC-MPR) which is a repository for millions of health and medical records of discharged and deceased veterans of all services during the twentieth century. (Records prior to WWI are in Washington, DC.) NPRC–MPR also stores medical treatment records of retirees from all services, as well as records for dependents and other people treated at military medical facilities. Information from the records is made available upon written request (with signature and date) to the extent allowed by law. This site is provided for those seeking information regarding military personnel, health and medical records stored at NPRC–MPR.

The process requires the completion of the Standard Form 180; this contains complete instructions for preparing and submitting requests. Note: All requests must be in writing, signed and mailed to the address shown below:

National Personnel Records Center
1 Archives Drive
St. Louis, Missouri 63138

Personal and Professional References

During the application process, personal and professional references are requested. These references must be contacted. In most cases, they provide good references or the applicant would not have listed them. Ask these contacts if they know anyone else who also knows the applicant. If the reference provides names and contact information for other people who know the applicant, contact them and obtain additional references. This will provide more insight into the applicant's background.

Residence Inquiry

When conducting a full background investigation, a residency inquiry may be conducted in the field. The goal is to determine where applicants have lived and whether they were living within their reported means based on salaries and their lifestyles and, additionally, to obtain references form landlords and neighbors.

Verify the dates of residence, whether rent was paid promptly if applicant was not a home owner, the condition of the property, and why the applicant moved. Interaction with neighbors, any evidence of criminal activity, positive community activity, and lifestyle can also be determined by a residence inquiry.

Family

It is permissible to conduct an inquiry of the applicant's family if family members will have access to company-protected information. Family members may present a conflict based on their positions in life and in the work force. Spouse and dependent children should be vetted to insure that there are no threats from possible blackmail, national security issues, or foreign governments.

Medical

The applicant's medical records can be reviewed only after a conditional offer of employment is made according to the American with Disabilities Act. The company can also require a physical and psychological examination. The primary goal is to ensure that the applicant is physically and mentally able to perform the duties of the position.

Any mental issues need to be explored to determine if the medical condition would lead to a situation where the individual might take part in industrial espionage and/or compromise company-protected information. All findings of the medical exam must be considered in relationship to possible industrial espionage.

Internet Search

A new focus to background investigation is conducting an Internet search of the applicant to see what links and photographs may be uncovered. Links such as Google, My Face, LinkedIn, and Twitter should be explored. The individual's name can also be run through various search engines to see if something appears.

Polygraph

The polygraph is an excellent tool for background employment investigations; however, remember that it is a violation of federal law to use the polygraph for pre-employment background investigations in the private sector with the exception of the private drug industry in the United States. Public law enforcement and the federal government can use the polygraph during the application process for their employees.

The polygraph is actually an instrument that trained professionals can read to determine whether an individual is telling the truth or lying. The polygraph has four to six sensors attached to the machine. The free end is attached to the subject. The polygraph machine has a strip of paper which prints out what the sensors are detecting. This graph on the strip of paper is what the polygraph interpreter will read to get the results of the test.

The person to be tested is seated next to a table on which the polygraph rests. The interpreter attaches the sensors to the individual. One sensor measures perspiration and another measures heart rate. A third sensor monitors blood pressure while the fourth detects a person's breathing rate. The interviewer takes his or her seat and gets the machine ready. The interviewer asks the suspect several general questions such as "Is your name John?" or "Are you 30 years old?" These are called baseline questions. Base questions require yes or no answers and these answers give the interviewer a guide to determine when the subject is telling the truth. When finished with the base questions, the interviewer asks the "bait" questions whose answers are pivotal in determining the truth. When finished, the interviewer unhooks the subject from the sensors and reviews the strip of paper from the machine.

The interviewer will use the base questions as the truth. When the interviewer sees an increase in perspiration, heart rate, blood pressure, or respiratory rate, he knows that the subject was lying when answering that particular question. The increase shows up on the graph as a larger line. He or she then prepares a report based on the findings from reading the strip of paper from the interview. There is no formula to determine whether the subject is lying or telling the truth. It is solely based on the interpretation by the one administering the polygraph. This is why polygraphs are not admissible in a court of law and are not permitted except for law enforcement and those going for US government security clearances for the prevention of espionage.

Periodic and Promotion Update Counterespionage Investigation

After an applicant is hired, a periodic or promotional investigation may be conducted. This occurs if the person has had access to protected information and there is concern that he or she may be involved in espionage. It may also be routine as a preventive measure for individuals with access to protected information.

All individuals with access to company protected information should have an updated background investigation every five years. This is an excellent tool in preventing espionage or identifying a threat.

A counterespionage update investigation should also be conducted when a current employee is being promoted or duties changed so that he or she will now have access to company-protected information and had no access in the past.

Non-Disclosure Non-Competitive Agreements

Non-disclosure agreements are utilized to protect organizations from the unauthorized disclosure of protected and or confidential company information from current or former employees and provides for a civil penalty for such disclosure either during employment or after leaving employment with the organization. There still could be criminal action if the information released was stolen and considered espionage.

The following sample non-disclosure agreement provides an overview of what should be included. The organization's legal staff should develop a non-disclosure agreement form to meet the specific needs of the organization.

SAMPLE EMPLOYEE NON-DISCLOSURE AGREEMENT

This Agreement is entered into this ___ day of ___, 200__ by and between __ with offices at __ (hereinafter "Recipient") and __, with offices at __ (hereinafter "Discloser").

WHEREAS Discloser possesses certain ideas and information relating to __ that is confidential and proprietary to Discloser (hereinafter "Confidential Information"); and

WHEREAS the Recipient is willing to receive disclosure of the Confidential Information pursuant to the terms of this Agreement for the purpose of _____:

NOW THEREFORE, in consideration for the mutual undertakings of the Discloser and the Recipient under this Agreement, the parties agree as follows:

1. Disclosure. Discloser agrees to disclose, and Receiver agrees to receive the Confidential Information.

2. Confidentiality.

2.1 No Use. Recipient agrees not to use the Confidential Information in any way, or to manufacture or test any product embodying Confidential Information, except for the purpose set forth above.

2.2 No Disclosure. Recipient agrees to use its best efforts to prevent and protect the Confidential Information, or any part thereof, from disclosure to any person other than Recipient's employees having a need for disclosure in connection with Recipient's authorized use of the Confidential Information.

2.3 Protection of Secrecy. Recipient agrees to take all steps reasonably necessary to protect the secrecy of the Confidential Information, and to prevent the Confidential Information from falling into the public domain or into the possession of unauthorized persons.

3. Limits on Confidential Information. Confidential Information shall not be deemed proprietary and the Recipient shall have no obligation with respect to such information where the information:

(a) was known to Recipient prior to receiving any of the Confidential Information from Discloser;

(b) has become publicly known through no wrongful act of Recipient;

(c) was received by recipient without breach of this agreement from a third party without restriction as to the use and disclosure of the information;

(d) was independently developed by Recipient without use of the Confidential Information; or

(e) was ordered to be publicly released by the requirement of a government agency.

4. Ownership of Confidential Information. Recipient agrees that all Confidential Information shall remain the property of Discloser, and that Discloser may use such Confidential Information for any purpose without obligation to Recipient. Nothing contained herein shall be construed as granting or implying any transfer of rights to Recipient in the Confidential Information, or any patents or other intellectual property protecting or relating to the Confidential Information.

5. Term and Termination. The obligations of this Agreement shall be continuing until the confidential Information disclosed to Recipient is no longer confidential.

6. Survival of Rights and Obligations. This Agreement shall be binding upon, inure to the benefit of, and be enforceable by (a) Discloser, its successors, and assigns; and (b) Recipient, its successors and assigns.

IN WITNESS WHEREOF, the parties have executed this agreement effective as of the date first written above.

DISCLOSER (_____) RECIPIENT (_____)

Signed: _____ Signed: _____

Print Name: _____ Print Name: _____

Title: _____ Title: _____

Date: _____ Date: _____

A non-competitive agreement is used to prevent a former employee from taking his or her knowledge from the company to a competitor. As it relates to espionage, the non-compete agreement can prevent an employee from revealing confidential and protected information. The following sample non-competitive can be used to prevent such situations and allow for civil recourse if the agreement is violated.

SAMPLE EMPLOYEE NON-COMPETE AGREEMENT

For good consideration and as an inducement for _____ (Company) to employ _____ (Employee), the undersigned Employee hereby agrees not to directly or indirectly compete with the business of the Company and its successors and assigns during the period of employment and for a period of ___ years following termination of employment and notwithstanding the cause or reason for termination.

The term "not compete" as used herein shall mean that the Employee shall not own, manage, operate, consult or be employed in a business substantially similar to, or competitive with, the present business of the Company or such other business activity in which the Company may substantially engage during the term of employment.

The Employee acknowledges that the Company shall or may in reliance of this agreement provide Employee access to trade secrets, customers and other confidential data and good will. Employee agrees to retain said information as confidential and not to use said information on his or her own behalf or disclose same to any third party.

This non-compete agreement shall extend only for a radius of ____ miles from the present location of the Company and shall be in full force and effect for ____ years, commencing with the date of employment termination.

This agreement shall be binding upon and inure to the benefit of the parties, their successors, assigns, and personal representatives.

Signed this ____ day of _____ 20____.

_____

Company

_____

Employee

Employee Exit Interview

An exit interview serves two purposes. First, it can be a valuable method of gathering information from departing employees concerning why they are leaving and their feeling toward the organization. Second, it can be utilized to ensure that employees surrender company equipment.

Company property needs to be returned during this interview, if not collected before. Returned items such as the employee's identification badge, laptop, mobile smart phone, company credit card, files, and any other portable physical items that the employee routinely used off company premises need to be accounted for and returned.

Below are suggested questions to ask during the exit interview:

- Why have you decided to leave the company?
- Have you shared your concerns with anyone in the company prior to deciding to leave?
- Was a single event responsible for your decision to leave?
- What does your new company offer that encouraged you to accept their offer and leave this company?
- What do you value about the company?
- What did you dislike about the company?
- What did you like most about your job?

- What did you dislike about your job? What would you change about your job?
- What would you recommend to help us create a better workplace?
- Do the policies and procedures of the company help to create a well-managed, consistent, and fair workplace in which expectations are clearly defined?
- Describe the qualities and characteristics of the person who is most likely to succeed in this company.
- Do you have any recommendations regarding our compensation, benefits and other reward and recognition efforts?
- What would make you consider working for this company again in the future? Would you recommend the company as a good place to work to your friends and family?
- Can you offer any other comments that will enable us to understand why you are leaving, how we can improve, and what we can do to become a better company?

During this interview the non-disclosure and non-competitive agreements need to be reviewed and the employee reminded of the requirement of those agreements. The legal ramification of the agreements, if not followed, needs to be reviewed with the employee.

End the exit interview meeting on a positive note. Commit to using the information provided to improve your workplace. Wish your employee success in his or her new endeavor. End the exit interview graciously.

Bibliography

Association of Certified Fraud Examiners (2000). *Corporate Espionage*. Austin, TX: Association of Certified Fraud Examiners.
Baker, P. & Benny, D. J. (2012). *Complete Guide to Physical Security*. Boca Raton, FL:CRC Press.
Central Intelligence Agency (2012). *Factbook*. Washington, DC: U.S. Government Printing Office.
Defense Security Service (2013). Retrieved from http://www.dss.mil/
Director of Central Intelligence Directive 1/21 *Manual for Physical Security Standards for Sensitive Compartmented Information Facilities* (1994). Washington, DC: U.S. Government Printing Office.
Federal Bureau of Investigation (2013). Retrieved from http://www.fbi.gov/scams-safety/registry.
Fischer, R. J. & Green, G. (2004). *Introduction to Security* (7th ed). Burlington, MA: Elsevier.

Heims, P. (1982). *Countering Industrial Espionage.* Surrey, UK: 20th Century Security Education.

Johnson, W.M. (2007). *Business Espionage.* Shoreline, WA: Questor Group.

Kovacich, G.L & Halibozek, E.P. (2004). *The Manager's Handbook for Corporate Security.*

Martin, S. (2005) *Business Intelligence and Corporate Espionage.* Boston, MA: Pearson.

National Archives (2013) Retrieved from http://www.archives.gov/st-louis/military-personnel/

The National Counterintelligence Center (2011). Annual Report to Congress on Foreign Economic Collection and Industrial Espionage. Washington, DC: U.S. Government Printing Office.

Office of National Intelligence (2013). Retrieved from http://www.intelligence.gov/about-the-intelligence-community.

Richelson, J. T. (1999) *The US Intelligence Community.* Boulder, CO: Westview Press.

Heims, P. (1982). *Countering Industrial Espionage.* Surrey, UK: 20th Century Security Education.

Winker, I. (1997) *Corporate Espionage.* New York, NY: Prima Publishing.

9

COUNTERESPIONAGE RESOURCES

Private Professional Intelligence Organizations

Private professional intelligence organizations and associations are excellent sources of information related to industrial espionage and counterespionage methods. Through such organizational web pages, magazines, journals, and newsletters, valuable information can be obtained.

The organizational websites also provide counterespionage training, seminars, workshops and professional certifications. Memberships in such organizations are also excellent sources of networking and the exchange of valuable security and counterespionage information.

Association of Former Intelligence Officers

In 1975, the Association of Retired Intelligence Officers was formed. In 1978, the name of the organization was changed to the Association of Former Intelligence Officers to reflect a pool of members who were not necessarily retired. This widened the pool of eligible members and reflects the current dynamic membership. The Association of Former Intelligence Officers has grown to more than 5,000 members with twenty-four active chapters across the United States.

A membership in the Intelligence Community Associations Network, the Association of Former Intelligence Officers is more than a professional or fraternal organization. Its distinguishing mission is educational; it reaches out to the public and explains what intelligence organizations do, and helps build a nation-wide constituency for intelligence as a profession.

The mission of the Association of Former Intelligence Officers is to build a public constituency for a sound, healthy and capable US intelligence system. Our focus on education fosters an understanding of the important role of intelligence in national security and nurtures interest by students in careers in the many fields offered by US intelligence

Agencies. This includes the role of supporting intelligence activities in US policy, diplomacy, strategy, security, and defense. The Association of Former Intelligence Officers focuses on understanding the critical need for effective counterintelligence and security against foreign, political, technological, or economic espionage as well as covert, clandestine, and overt counterterrorist or criminal operations threatening US security, the national infrastructure or corporate and individual safety.

6723 Whittier Avenue, Suite 200
McLean, Virginia 22101-4533
Telephone: 703-790-0320
Email: afio@afio.com
Web page: http://www.afio.com

Business Espionage Controls and Countermeasures Association

The Business Espionage Controls and Countermeasures Association (BECCA) began in 1986 as an informal network of controls and countermeasures experts brought together by Dr. William M. Johnson, founder and executive director. BECCA is based on original concepts, training materials, and certification programs to which he retains the exclusive copyrights.

Dr. Johnson published the first issue of the BECCA newsletter, *The Business Espionage Report,* in 1986, and identified the four faces of business espionage (pretext attacks, computer abuse, technical surveillance, and undercover operations) in one of his first research projects.

BECCA was incorporated on June 22, 1990 as the Business Espionage Controls and Countermeasures Association (BECCA), a nonprofit organization in Washington State.

"The purpose of the association is to research and exchange information about business espionage controls and countermeasures; to establish and encourage a code of ethics within the profession, and to promote our professional image within the business community through a Certified Confidentiality Officer (CCO) Program. It is organized exclusively for, and will be operated for scientific, literary and educational purposes." The Certified Confidentiality Officer Program is approved by the DOD, the Higher Education Coordinating Board of Washington State, and the Department of Veterans Affairs."

Dr. Johnson took part in a research project cosponsored by the US Departments of Labor and Education to "adopt a strategy to establish job-related (and industry-specific) skill standards, built around core proficiencies, and to develop skill certificates to accompany these standards." (*Federal Register*, Vol.57, March 18, 1992.) The BECCA Certified Confidentiality Program is based on this research, and was cited at the National Educational Leadership Conference in 1992 as follows:

"The US Department of Education is impressed with the BECCA Certified Confidentiality Officer (CCO) Program. We are especially impressed that a private organization has gone ahead on its own with this much-needed project." (Dept. of Education, Business and Educational Standards)

Professional certification validates your training and experience in your present career and provides a bridge to the future if your career is in transition. BECCA's Certified Confidentiality Program has been updated and restructured to fit the needs of a wide range of busy professionals who already have some security training and experience. It is responsive to different adult learning styles and is free from gender, age, racial, ethnic, and other forms of discrimination.

The Certified Confidentiality Program is not a correspondence course; it is a certification program based on accepted educational standards. To obtain the Certified Confidentiality Officer credential, candidates are required to document their education, related experience, and skill standards in performing security surveys, audits, and inspections. CCO designation is awarded to individuals who complete all requirements and pass a proctored exam which covers:

Putting the spy world in perspective - 20%
The personal side of business espionage - 17%
Pretext attacks - 10%
Computer abuse - 15%
Technical surveillance - 18%
Undercover attacks - 10%
Planning controls and countermeasures programs - 10%
Publications
    The CD 101 Questions & Answers About Business Espionage by
       Dr. William M. Johnson and this text are used to prepare

candidates for the CCO Examination in both the public and private sectors. The exam is offered at a number of test sites in the US and elsewhere.

The CD of Best Practice Guidelines in Business Espionage Controls & Countermeasures, by Spyridon Kyriakakis, Jason Dibley, Jose Abreu and John Kanalis, is included in the CCO Program.

P.O. Box 55582
Shoreline, Washington 98155-0582
Telephone: 717-238-1740
Email: Office@BECCA-online.org
Web page: http://becca-online.org/beccahome.html

International Association for Intelligence Education

IAFIE was formed in June 2004 as a result of a gathering of sixty-plus intelligence studies trainers and educators. This group, from various intelligence disciplines including national security, law enforcement and competitive intelligence, recognized the need for a professional association that would span their diverse disciplines and provide a catalyst and resources for their development and that of intelligence studies.

Purpose Expanding research, knowledge, and professional development in intelligence education; providing a forum for the exchange of ideas and information for those interested in and concerned with intelligence education; advancing the intelligence profession by setting standards, building resources, and sharing knowledge in intelligence studies; fostering relationships and cultivating cooperation among intelligence professionals in academia, business, and government; developing, disseminating, and promoting theory, curricula, methodologies, techniques, and best practices for pure and applied intelligence; serving as a liaison between other professional organizations and centers of excellence.

P.O. Box 10508
Erie, Pennsylvania 16514
Telephone: 814-824-2131
Web page: http://www.iafie.org/

International Spy Museum

This is the only public museum in the United States dedicated to espionage and the only one in the world to provide a global perspective on an all-but-invisible profession that has shaped history and continues to have a significant impact on world events.

The International Spy Museum features the largest collection of international espionage artifacts ever placed on public display. Many of these objects are being seen by the public for the first time. These artifacts illuminate the work of famous spies and pivotal espionage actions as well as help bring to life the strategies and techniques of the men and women behind some of the most secretive espionage missions in world history.

The mission of the International Spy Museum is to educate the public about espionage in an engaging way and to provide a context that fosters understanding of its important role in and impact on current and historic events. The museum focuses on human intelligence and reveals the role spies have played in world events throughout history. It is committed to the apolitical presentation of the history of espionage in order to provide visitors with unbiased, accurate information.

800 F Street NW
Washington, DC 20004
Telephone: 202-393-7798
Email: membership@spymuseum.org
Web page: http://www.spymuseum.org/visit/

Naval Intelligence Professionals

The goal of the Naval Intelligence Professionals (NIP) is to further the knowledge of the art of maritime intelligence, and to provide a vehicle whereby present and former Naval Intelligence professionals may be kept informed of developments in the Naval Intelligence community and of the activities and whereabouts of past shipmates. Founded in 1985, NIP is a nonprofit organization incorporated to enhance awareness of the mission and vital functions of the Naval Intelligence community, as well as to foster camaraderie among Naval Intelligence professionals. It is an association of active duty, retired, and reserve officers, enlisted personnel, and civilians who serve or have served within the Naval Intelligence community, as well as those in certain other categories who qualify as nonvoting subscribers.

P.O. Box 11579
Burke, Virginia 22009-1579
Email: navintpro@aol.com
Web page: http://navintpro.net/

Society of Competitive Intelligence Professionals

The Strategic and Competitive Intelligence Professionals (SCIP), formerly the Society of Competitive Intelligence Professionals, is a global nonprofit membership organization for everyone involved in creating and managing business knowledge. Their mission is to enhance the success of its members through leadership, education, advocacy, and networking. SCIP provides education and networking opportunities for business professionals working in the rapidly growing field of competitive intelligence (the legal and ethical collection and analysis of information regarding the capabilities, vulnerabilities, and intentions of business competitors). Since being established in 1986, SCIP has chapters around the world with individual members in nations around the globe.

P.O. Box 277
Falls Church, Virginia 22040
Telephone: 703-739-0696
E-mail: info@scip.org
Web page: http://www.scip.org

Private Professional Security Organizations

Private professional security organizations and association are exceptional sources of information related to security which is essential to the counterespionage program. Through their web pages, magazines, journals, and newsletters, valuable information can be obtained.

These organizations also provide security training, seminars, workshops and professional certifications. Memberships in such organizations are also excellent sources of networking and the exchange of valuable security information.

ASIS International

ASIS International is the preeminent society for security profession-als. Founded in 1955 as the American Society for Industrial Security, the organization is dedicated to security professionals by developing educational programs and publications that address security interests. This includes the annual seminar and exhibits. ASIS International also publishes the industry's number one magazine *Security Management.* The ASIS Commission on Standards and Guidelines has developed various security management standards and guidelines that are used by the security profession.

ASIS Certifications   ASIS administers three internationally accredited certification programs. The Certified Protection Professional (CPP) board certification in security management is recognized as the highest designation accorded a security practitioner. Two specialty certifications are also available; these are the Professional Certified Investigator (PCI) and the Physical Security Professional (PSP).

1625 Prince Street
Alexandria, Virginia 22314
Telephone: 702-519-6200
Email: asis@asisonline.org
Web page: http://www.asisonline.org

Association of British Investigators

Formed in 1913, the Association of British Investigators (ABI) has been upholding professional standards in England for a century. The ABI campaigns tirelessly for regulation in the private investigative profession and promotes excellence, integrity, and professionalism within its membership.

295/297 Church Street
Blackpool, Lancashire
FY1 3PJ

England
Telephone: 012532975
Email: info@theaib.org.uk
Web page: http://www.theabi.org.uk

Association of Certified Fraud Examiners

The ACFE is the world's largest anti-fraud organization and premier provider of anti-fraud training and education. With nearly 65,000 members, the ACFE is reducing business fraud worldwide and inspiring public confidence in the integrity and objectivity within the profession. The Certified Fraud Examiner (CFE) credential denotes proven expertise in fraud prevention, detection and deterrence. CFEs around the world help protect the global economy by uncovering fraud and implementing processes to prevent fraud from occurring in the first place.

The Gregor Building
716 West Avenue
Austin, Texas 78701-2727
Telephone: 800-245-3321
Email: memberservices@acfe.com
Web page: http://www.acfe.com/

National Council of Investigation and Security Services

The objective of the council is to monitor national legislative and regulatory activities affecting the investigation and security industry. A substantial part of the council's activities shall be to assist, advise, inform and influence legislation and to develop and encourage the practice of high standards of personal and professional conduct among those persons serving in the investigation and security industry; to promote the purpose and effectiveness of investigation and security companies by any and all means consistent with the public interest; to promote the private investigation and security industry; to educate members and the public in the advancement, improvement and uses of investigation and security services; to assist local, state, or regional groups of investigation and security companies in the common endeavor to advance and promote the investigation and security industry; to provide the opportunity for the exchange of experiences and opinions through discussion, study, the Internet and publications; to cooperate in courses of study for the benefit of persons desiring to fit themselves for positions in the investigation and security industry, and to hold meetings and conferences for the mutual improvement and education of our members; to acquire, preserve, and to disseminate data and valuable information relative to the functions and accomplishments of investigation and security companies. Subject to prior approval of the board, the council may take a position and express an opinion on issues directly and generally affecting the investigation and security industry as such; provided, however, that no action shall be taken on such matters as clearly fall solely within the purview of an individual investigation or security company or a distinct group of investigation or security companies.

7501 Sparrows Point Blvd.
Baltimore, Maryland 21219-1927
Telephone: 800-445-8408
Email: inquire@nciss.org
Web page: www.ncis.org

World Association of Detectives

The World Association of Detectives was founded in 1925. In 1950, the World Secret Service Association, Inc. was formed as a joint venture by the combined memberships of the International Secret Service Association (founded in 1921) and the World Association of Detectives. At the annual conference in August 1966 in San Antonio, Texas, the present name was unanimously approved by amendment, reverting to the name of World Association of Detectives.

7501 Sparrows Point Blvd.
Baltimore, Maryland 21219-1927
Telephone: 443-982-4585
Email: wad1924@comcast.net
Web page: http://www.wad.net/site/pages/home.cgi

US Government Security and Intelligence Agencies

Defense Security Service

Mission   Provide the Department of Defense (DoD) with a security center of excellence for the professionalization of the security community and be the premier provider of security education and training for the DoD and industry. The CDSE will furnish unparalleled development, delivery, and exchange of security knowledge to ensure a high-performing workforce capable of addressing our nation's security challenges.

Vision   To be the premier provider and center of excellence for security training, professionalization, education, research, and multimedia production for the DoD and the defense industrial base.

Divisions   The Education Division develops education courses and workshops for DoD security professionals who are advancing their professional growth. This division is responsible for the development of education courses for advanced security studies in support of the Security Professional Education Development Certification Program. The Education Division is also responsible for facilitating the evaluation of SETA training and education courses for college credit equivalencies.

The Training Division provides security training to DoD and other US Government personnel, employees of US government contractors, and when sponsored by authorized DoD components, employees of foreign governments. The Training Division creates, collaborates, and facilitates delivery of quality training across the industrial, information, personnel, and physical security disciplines, as well as other security related areas such as special access programs. Training is delivered through a variety of formats to include resident courses conducted at the DSS facility in Linthicum, MD; mobile courses delivered at activities located within or outside the United States, and distance learning courses, audio podcasts, and performance support tools accessed online via the CDSE website and Learning Management System, STEPP. The training division also operates the Defense Security Service Academy (DSSA); the

DSSA provides security training for industrial security professionals within the Defense Security Service.

The Multimedia Productions Division is responsible for developing, implementing, and maintaining the Security Professional Education Development (SPED) Certification Program, including maintaining DoD security skill standards, developing and providing career services for DoD security professionals, and supporting the DoD Security Training Council (DSTC). The Division is also responsible for communication and liaison with DoD security community stakeholders/customers and sponsorship/support of security-themed workshops, conferences, and events.

Defense Security Service
27130 Telegraph Road
Quantico, Virginia 22134
571-305-6751
571-305-6752
http://www.dss.mil/index.html

Federal Bureau of Investigation

FBI Mission   As an intelligence-driven and a threat-focused national security organization with both intelligence and law enforcement responsibilities, the mission of the FBI is to protect and defend the United States against terrorist and foreign intelligence threats, to uphold and enforce the criminal laws of the United States, and to provide leadership and criminal justice services to federal, state, municipal, and international agencies and partners.

Priorities   The FBI focuses on threats that challenge the foundations of American society or involve dangers too large or complex for any local or state authority to handle alone. In executing the following priorities, the FBI—as both a national security and law enforcement organization—will produce and use intelligence to protect the nation from threats and to bring to justice those who violate the law:

1. Protect the United States from terrorist attack
2. Protect the United States against foreign intelligence operations and espionage
3. Protect the United States against cyber-based attacks and high-technology crimes
4. Combat public corruption at all levels
5. Protect civil rights
6. Combat transnational/national criminal organizations and enterprises
7. Combat major white-collar crime
8. Combat significant violent crime
9. Support federal, state, local and international partners
10. Upgrade technology to successfully perform the FBI's mission

FBI Headquarters
935 Pennsylvania Avenue, NW
Washington, DC 20535-0001
202-324-3000
http://www.fbi.gov/

Appendix A

Espionage Act 1917

Section 1

That
(a) whoever, for the purpose of obtaining information respecting the national defence with intent or reason to believe that the information to be obtained is to be used to the injury of the United States, or to the advantage of any foreign nation, goes upon, enters, flies over, or otherwise obtains information, concerning any vessel, aircraft, work of defence, navy yard, naval station, submarine base, coaling station, fort, battery, torpedo station, dockyard, canal, railroad, arsenal, camp, factory, mine, telegraph, telephone, wireless, or signal station, building, office, or other place connected with the national defence, owned or constructed, or in progress of construction by the United States or under the control or the United States, or of any of its officers or agents, or within the exclusive jurisdiction of the United States, or any place in which any vessel, aircraft, arms, munitions, or other materials or instruments for use in time of war are being made, prepared, repaired. or stored, under any contract or agreement with the United States, or with any person on behalf of

the United States, or otherwise on behalf of the United States, or any prohibited place within the meaning of section six of this title; or

(b) whoever for the purpose aforesaid, and with like intent or reason to believe, copies, takes, makes, or obtains, or attempts, or induces or aids another to copy, take, make, or obtain, any sketch, photograph, photographic negative, blue print, plan, map, model, instrument, appliance, document, writing or note of anything connected with the national defence; or

(c) whoever, for the purpose aforesaid, receives or obtains or agrees or attempts or induces or aids another to receive or obtain from any other person, or from any source whatever, any document, writing, code book, signal book, sketch, photograph, photographic negative, blue print, plan, map, model, instrument, appliance, or note, of anything connected with the national defence, knowing or having reason to believe, at the time he receives or obtains, or agrees or attempts or induces or aids another to receive or obtain it, that it has been or will be obtained, taken, made or disposed of by any person contrary to the provisions of this title; or

(d) whoever, lawfully or unlawfully having possession of, access to, control over, or being entrusted with any document, writing, code book, signal book, sketch, photograph, photographic negative, blue print, plan, map, model, instrument, appliance, or note relating to the national defence, willfully communicates or transmits or attempts to communicate or transmit the same and fails to deliver it on demand to the officer or employee of the United States entitled to receive it; or

(e) whoever, being entrusted with or having lawful possession or control of any document, writing, code book, signal book, sketch, photograph, photographic negative, blue print, plan, map, model, note, or information, relating to the national defence, through gross negligence permits the same to be removed from its proper place of custody or delivered to anyone in violation of his trust, or to be list, stolen, abstracted, or destroyed, shall be punished by a fine of not more than $10,000, or by imprisonment for not more than two years, or both.

Section 2

Whoever, with intent or reason to believe that it is to be used to the injury or the United States or to the advantage of a foreign nation, communicated, delivers, or transmits, or attempts to, or aids, or induces another to, communicate, deliver or transmit, to any foreign government, or to any faction or party or military or naval force within a foreign country, whether recognized or unrecognized by the United States, or to any representative, officer, agent, employee, subject, or citizen thereof, either directly or indirectly and document, writing, code book, signal book, sketch, photograph, photographic negative, blue print, plan, map, model, note, instrument, appliance, or information relating to the national defence, shall be punished by imprisonment for not more than twenty years.

Provided, That whoever shall violate the provisions of subsection (a) of this section in time of war shall be punished by death or by imprisonment for not more than thirty years; and (b) whoever, in time of war, with intent that the same shall be communicated to the enemy, shall collect, record, publish or communicate, or attempt to elicit any information with respect to the movement, numbers, description, condition, or disposition of any of the armed forces, ships, aircraft, or war materials of the United States, or with respect to the plans or conduct, or supposed plans or conduct of any naval of military operations, or with respect to any works or measures undertaken for or connected with, or intended for the fortification of any place, or any other information relating to the public defence, which might be useful to the enemy, shall be punished by death or by imprisonment for not more than thirty years.

Section 3

Whoever, when the United States is at war, shall willfully make or convey false reports or false statements with intent to interfere with the operation or success of the military or naval forces of the United States or to promote the success of its enemies and whoever when the United States is at war, shall willfully cause or attempt to cause insubordination, disloyalty, mutiny, refusal of duty, in the military or naval forces of the United States, or shall willfully obstruct the recruiting or enlistment service of the United States, to the injury of the service or of the United States, shall be punished by a fine of not more than $10,000 or imprisonment for not more than twenty years, or both.

Section 4

If two or more persons conspire to violate the provisions of section two or three of this title, and one or more of such persons does any act to effect the object of the conspiracy, each of the parties to such conspiracy shall be punished as in said sections provided in the case of the doing of the act the accomplishment of which is the object of such conspiracy. Except as above provided conspiracies to commit offences under this title shall be punished as provided by section thirty-seven of the Act to codify, revise, and amend the penal laws of the United States approved March fourth, nineteen hundred and nine.

Section 5

Whoever harbours or conceals any person who he knows, or has reasonable grounds to believe or suspect, has committed, or is about to commit, an offence under this title shall be punished by a fine of not more than $10,000 or by imprisonment for not more than two years, or both.

Section 6

The President in time of war or in case of national emergency may by proclamation designate any place other than those set forth in subsection: (a) of section one hereof in which anything for the use of the Army or Navy is being prepared or constructed or stored as a prohibited place for the purpose of this title: Provided, That he shall determine that information with respect thereto would be prejudicial to the national defence.

Section 7

Nothing contained in this title shall be deemed to limit the jurisdiction of the general courts-martial, military commissions, or naval courts-martial under sections thirteen hundred and forty-two, thirteen hundred and forty-three, and sixteen hundred and twenty-four of the Revised Statutes as amended.

Section 8

The provisions of this title shall extend to all Territories, possessions, and places subject to the jurisdiction of the United States whether or not contiguous thereto, and offences under this title, when committed upon the high seas or elsewhere within the admiralty and maritime jurisdiction of the United States and outside the territorial limits thereof shall be punishable hereunder.

Section 9

The Act entitles "An Act to prevent the disclosure of national defence secrets," approved March third, nineteen hundred and eleven, is hereby repealed.

Appendix B

United States Economic Espionage Act of 1996

SECTION 1. SHORT TITLE.

This Act may be cited as the Economic Espionage Act of 1996.

TITLE I — PROTECTION OF TRADE SECRETS

SEC. 101. PROTECTION OF TRADE SECRETS.

(a) IN GENERAL - Title 18, United States Code, is amended by inserting after chapter 89 the following

CHAPTER 90 — PROTECTION OF TRADE SECRETS

Sec.

1831. Economic espionage.

1832. Theft of trade secrets.

1833. Exceptions to prohibitions.

1834. Criminal forfeiture.

1835. Orders to preserve confidentiality.

1836. Civil proceedings to enjoin violations.

1837. Conduct outside the United States.

1838. Construction with other laws.

1839. Definitions.

Sec. 1831. Economic espionage

(a) IN GENERAL - Whoever, intending or knowing that the offense will benefit any foreign government, foreign instrumentality, or foreign agent, knowingly—

(1) steals, or without authorization appropriates, takes, carries away, or conceals, or by fraud, artifice, or deception obtains a trade secret;

(2) without authorization copies, duplicates, sketches, draws, photographs, downloads, uploads, alters, destroys, photocopies, replicates, transmits, delivers, sends, mails, communicates, or conveys a trade secret;

(3) receives, buys, or possesses a trade secret, knowing the same to have been stolen or appropriated, obtained, or converted without authorization;

4) attempts to commit any offense described in any of paragraphs (1) through (3); or

(5) conspires with one or more other persons to commit any offense described in any of paragraphs (1) through (3), and one or more of such persons do any act to effect the object of the conspiracy, shall, except as provided in subsection (b), be fined not more than $500,000 or imprisoned not more than 15 years, or both.

(b) ORGANIZATIONS - Any organization that commits any offense described in subsection (a) shall be fined not more than $10,000,000.

Sec. 1832. Theft of trade secrets

(a) Whoever, with intent to convert a trade secret, that is related to or included in a product that is produced for or placed in interstate or foreign commerce, to the economic benefit of anyone other than the owner thereof, and intending or knowing that the offense will, injure any owner of that trade secret, knowingly—

(1) steals, or without authorization appropriates, takes, carries away, or conceals, or by fraud, artifice, or deception obtains such information;

(2) without authorization copies, duplicates, sketches, draws, photographs, downloads, uploads, alters, destroys, photocopies, replicates, transmits, delivers, sends, mails, communicates, or conveys such information;

(3) receives, buys, or possesses such information, knowing the same to have been stolen or appropriated, obtained, or converted without authorization;

(4) attempts to commit any offense described in paragraphs (1) through (3); or

(5) conspires with one or more other persons to commit any offense described in paragraphs (1) through (3), and one or more of such persons do any act to effect the object of the conspiracy, shall, except as provided in subsection (b), be fined under this title or imprisoned not more than 10 years, or both.

(b) Any organization that commits any offense described in subsection (a) shall be fined not more than $5,000,000.

Sec. 1833. Exceptions to prohibitions

This chapter does not prohibit—

(1) any otherwise lawful activity conducted by a governmental entity of the United States, a State, or a political subdivision of a State; or

(2) the reporting of a suspected violation of law to any governmental entity of the United States, a State, or a political subdivision of a State, if such entity has lawful authority with respect to that violation.

Sec. 1834. Criminal forfeiture

(a) The court, in imposing sentence on a person for a violation of this chapter, shall order, in addition to any other sentence imposed, that the person forfeit to the United States—

(1) any property constituting, or derived from, any proceeds the person obtained, directly or indirectly, as the result of such violation; and

(2) any of the person's property used, or intended to be used, in any manner or part, to commit or facilitate the commission of such violation, if the court in its discretion so determines, taking into consideration the nature, scope, and proportionality of the use of the property in the offense.

(b) Property subject to forfeiture under this section, any seizure and disposition thereof, and any administrative or judicial proceeding in relation thereto, shall be governed by section 413 of the Comprehensive Drug Abuse Prevention and Control Act of 1970 (21 U.S.C. 853), except for subsections (d) and (j) of such section, which shall not apply to forfeitures under this section.

Sec. 1835. Orders to preserve confidentiality

In any prosecution or other proceeding under this chapter, the court shall enter such orders and take such other action as may be necessary and appropriate to preserve the confidentiality of trade secrets, consistent with the requirements of the Federal Rules of Criminal and Civil Procedure, the Federal Rules of Evidence, and all other applicable laws. An interlocutory appeal by the United States shall lie from a decision or order of a district court authorizing or directing the disclosure of any trade secret.

Sec. 1836. Civil proceedings to enjoin violations

(a) The Attorney General may, in a civil action, obtain appropriate injunctive relief against any violation of this section.

(b) The district courts of the United States shall have exclusive original jurisdiction of civil actions under this subsection.

Sec. 1837. Applicability to conduct outside the United States

This chapter also applies to conduct occurring outside the United States if—

(1) the offender is a natural person who is a citizen or permanent resident alien of the United States, or an organization organized under the laws of the United States or a State or political subdivision thereof; or

(2) an act in furtherance of the offense was committed in the United States.

Sec. 1838. Construction with other laws

This chapter shall not be construed to preempt or displace any other remedies, whether civil or criminal, provided by United States Federal, State, commonwealth, possession, or territory law for the misappropriation of a trade secret, or to affect the otherwise lawful disclosure of information by any Government employee under section 552 of title 5 (commonly known as the Freedom of Information Act).

Sec. 1839. Definitions

As used in this chapter—

(1) the term 'foreign instrumentality' means any agency, bureau, ministry, component, institution, association, or any legal, commercial, or business organization, corporation, firm, or entity that is substantially owned, controlled, sponsored, commanded, managed, or dominated by a foreign government;

(2) the term 'foreign agent' means any officer, employee, proxy, servant, delegate, or representative of a foreign government;

(3) the term 'trade secret' means all forms and types of financial, business, scientific, technical, economic, or engineering information, including patterns, plans, compilations, program devices, formulas, designs, prototypes, methods, techniques, processes, procedures, programs, or codes, whether tangible or intangible, and whether or how stored, compiled, or memorialized physically, electronically, graphically, photographically, or in writing if—

(A) the owner thereof has taken reasonable measures to keep such information secret; and

(B) the information derives independent economic value, actual or potential, from not being generally known to, and not being readily ascertainable through proper means by, the public; and

(4) the term 'owner', with respect to a trade secret, means the person or entity in whom or in which rightful legal or equitable title to, or license in, the trade secret is reposed.

(b) CLERICAL AMENDMENT - The table of chapters at the beginning part I of title 18, United States Code, is amended by inserting after the item relating to chapter 89 the following:

(c) REPORTS - Not later than 2 years and 4 years after the date of the enactment of this Act, the Attorney General shall report to Congress on the amounts received and distributed from fines for offenses under this chapter deposited in the Crime Victims Fund established by section 1402 of the Victims of Crime Act of 1984 (42 U.S.C. 10601).

Appendix C

UNIFORM TRADE SECRETS ACT
WITH 1985 AMENDMENTS

SECTION 1. DEFINITIONS. As used in this [Act], unless the context requires otherwise

(1) "Improper means" includes theft, bribery, misrepresentation, breach or inducement of a breach of a duty to maintain secrecy, or espionage through electronic or other means;

(2) "Misappropriation" means:

(i) acquisition of a trade secret of another by a person who knows or has reason to know that the trade secret was acquired by improper means; or

(I) disclosure or use of a trade secret of another without express or implied consent by a person who

(A) used improper means to acquire knowledge of the trade secret; or

(B) at the time of disclosure or use, knew or had reason to know that his knowledge of the trade secret was

(I) derived from or through a person who had utilized improper means to acquire it;

(II) acquired under circumstances giving rise to a duty to maintain its secrecy or limit its use; or

(III) derived from or through a person who owed a duty to the person seeking relief to maintain its secrecy or limit its use; or

(C) before a material change of his [or her] position, knew or had reason to know that it was a trade secret and that knowledge of it had been acquired by accident or mistake.

(3) "Person" means a natural person, corporation, business trust, estate, trust, partnership, association, joint venture, government, governmental subdivision or agency, or any other legal or commercial entity.

(4) "Trade secret" means information, including a formula, pattern, compilation, program, device, method, technique, or process, that:

(i) derives independent economic value, actual or potential, from not being generally known to, and not being readily ascertainable by proper means by, other persons who can obtain economic value from its disclosure or use, and

(ii) is the subject of efforts that are reasonable under the circumstances to maintain its secrecy.

Comment: One of the broadly stated policies behind trade secret law is "the maintenance of standards of commercial ethics," *Kewanee Oil Co. v. Bicron Corp.*, 416 U.S. 470 (1974). The Restatement of Torts, Section 757, Comment (f), notes: "A complete catalogue of improper means is not possible," but Section 1(1) includes a partial listing.

Proper means include:

1. Discovery by independent invention;

2. Discovery by "reverse engineering", that is, by starting with the known product and working backward to find the method by which it was developed. The acquisition of the known product must, of course, also be by a fair and honest means, such as purchase of the item on the open market for reverse engineering to be lawful;

3. Discovery under a license from the owner of the trade secret;

4. Observation of the item in public use or on public display;

5. Obtaining the trade secret from published literature.

Improper means could include otherwise lawful conduct which is improper under the circumstances; e.g., an airplane overflight used as aerial reconnaissance to determine the competitor's plant layout during construction of the plant, *E. I. du Pont de Nemours & Co., Inc. v. Christopher*, 431 F.2d 1012 (CA5, 1970), cert. denied 400 U.S. 1024 (1970). Because the trade secret can be destroyed through public knowledge, the unauthorized disclosure of a trade secret is also a misappropriation.

The type of accident or mistake that can result in a misappropriation under Section 1(2)(ii)(C) involves conduct by a person seeking relief that does not constitute a failure of efforts that are reasonable under the circumstances to maintain its secrecy under Section 1(4)(ii).

The definition of "trade secret" contains a reasonable departure from the Restatement of Torts (First) definition which required that a trade secret be "continuously used in one's business." The broader definition in the proposed Act extends protection to a plaintiff who has not yet had an opportunity or acquired the means to put a trade secret to use. The definition includes information that has commercial value from a negative viewpoint, for example the results of lengthy and expensive research which proves that a certain process will not work could be of great value to a competitor.

Cf. Telex Corp. v. IBM Corp., 510 F.2d 894 (CA10, 1975) per curiam, cert. dismissed 423 U.S. 802 (1975) (liability imposed for developmental cost savings with respect to product not marketed). Because a trade secret need not be exclusive to confer a competitive advantage, different independent developers can acquire rights in the same trade secret.

The words "method, technique" are intended to include the concept of "know-how."

The language "not being generally known to and not being readily ascertainable by proper means by other persons" does not require that information be generally known to the public for trade secret rights to be lost. If the principal person or persons who can obtain economic benefit from information are aware of it, there is no trade secret. A method of casting metal, for example, may be unknown to the general public but readily known within the foundry industry.

Information is readily ascertainable if it is available in trade journals, reference books, or published materials. Often, the nature of a product lends itself to being readily copied as soon as it is available on the market. On the other hand, if reverse engineering is lengthy and expensive, a person who discovers the trade secret through reverse engineering can have a trade secret in the information obtained from reverse engineering.

Finally, reasonable efforts to maintain secrecy have been held to include advising employees of the existence of a trade secret, limiting access to a trade secret on "need to know basis," and controlling plant access. On the other hand, public disclosure of information through display, trade journal publications, advertising, or other carelessness can preclude protection.

The efforts required to maintain secrecy are those "reasonable under the circumstances." The courts do not require that extreme and unduly expensive procedures be taken to protect trade secrets against flagrant industrial espionage. See *E. I. du Pont de Nemours & Co., Inc. v. Christopher*, supra. It follows that reasonable use of a trade secret including controlled disclosure to employees and licensees is consistent with the requirement of relative secrecy.

SECTION 2. INJUNCTIVE RELIEF.

(a) Actual or threatened misappropriation may be enjoined. Upon application to the court, an injunction shall be terminated when the trade secret has ceased to exist, but the injunction may be continued for an additional reasonable period of time in order to eliminate commercial advantage that otherwise would be derived from the misappropriation.

(b) If the court determines that it would be unreasonable to prohibit future use In exceptional circumstances, an injunction may condition future use upon payment of a reasonable royalty for no longer than the period of time the for which use could have been prohibited. Exceptional circumstances include, but are not limited to, a material and prejudicial change of position prior to acquiring knowledge or reason to know of misappropriation that renders a prohibitive injunction inequitable.

(c) In appropriate circumstances, affirmative acts to protect a trade secret may be compelled by court order.

Comment

Injunctions restraining future use and disclosure of misappropriated trade secrets frequently are sought. Although punitive perpetual injunctions have been granted, e.g., *Elcor Chemical Corp. v. Agri-Sul, Inc.*, 494 SW2d 204 (Tex. Civ. App. 1973), Section 2(a) of this Act adopts the position of the trend of authority limiting the duration of injunctive relief to the extent of the temporal advantage over good faith competitors gained by a misappropriator. See, e.g., *K-2 Ski Co. v. Head Ski Co., Inc.*, 506 F.2d 471 (CA9, 1974) (maximum appropriate duration of both temporary and permanent injunctive relief is period of time it would have taken defendant to discover trade secrets lawfully through either independent development or reverse engineering of plaintiff's products).

The general principle of Section 2(a) and (b) is that an injunction should last for as long as is necessary, but no longer than is necessary, to eliminate the commercial advantage or "lead time" with respect to good faith competitors that a person has obtained through misappropriation. Subject to any additional period of restraint necessary to negate lead time, an injunction accordingly should terminate when a former trade secret becomes either generally known to good faith competitors or generally knowable to them because of the lawful availability of products that can be reverse engineered to reveal a trade secret.

For example, assume that A has a valuable trade secret of which B and C, the other industry members, are originally unaware. If B subsequently misappropriates the trade secret and is enjoined from use, but C later lawfully reverse engineers the trade secret, the injunction restraining B is subject to termination as soon as B's lead time has been dissipated. All of the persons who could derive economic value from use of the information are now aware of it, and there is no longer a trade secret under Section 1(4). It would be anti-competitive to continue to restrain B after any lead time that B had derived from misappropriation had been removed.

If a misappropriator either has not taken advantage of lead time or good faith competitors already have caught up with a misappropriator at the time that a case is decided, future disclosure and use of a former trade secret by a misappropriator will not damage a trade secret owner and no injunctive restraint of future disclosure and use is appropriate. See, e.g., *Northern Petrochemical Co. v. Tomlinson*, 484 F.2d 1057 (CA7, 1973) (affirming trial court's denial of preliminary injunction in part because an explosion at its plant prevented an alleged misappropriator from taking advantage of lead time); *Kubik, Inc. v. Hull*, 185 USPQ 391 (Mich. App. 1974) (discoverability of trade secret by lawful reverse engineering made by injunctive relief punitive rather than compensatory).

Section 2(b) deals with a distinguishable the special situation in which future use by a misappropriator will damage a trade secret owner but an injunction against future use nevertheless is unreasonable under the particular situation and inappropriate due to exceptional circumstances of a case. Exceptional circumstances include the existence of an overriding public interest which requires the denial of a prohibitory injunction against future damaging use and a person's reasonable reliance upon acquisition of a misappropriated trade secret in good faith and without reason to know of its prior misappropriation that would be prejudiced by a prohibitory injunction against future damaging use. *Republic Aviation Corp. v. Schenk*, 152 USPQ 830 (NY Sup. Ct. 1967) illustrates the public interest justification for withholding prohibitory injunctive relief. The court considered that enjoining a misappropriator from supplying the U.S. with an aircraft weapons control system would have endangered military personnel in Viet Nam. The prejudice to a good faith third party justification for withholding prohibitory injunctive relief can arise upon a trade secret owner's notification to a good faith third party that the third party has knowledge of a trade secret as a result of misappropriation by another. This notice suffices to make the third party a misappropriator thereafter under Section 1(2)(ii)(B)(I). In weighing an aggrieved person's interests and the interests of a third party who has relied in good faith upon his or her ability to utilize information, a court may conclude that restraining future use of the information by the third party is unwarranted. With respect to innocent acquirers of misappropriated trade secrets, Section 2(b) is consistent with the principle of 4 Restatement of Torts (First) § 758(b) (1939), but rejects the Restatement's literal conferral of absolute immunity upon all third parties who have paid value in good faith for a trade secret misappropriated by another. The position taken by the Uniform Act is supported by *Forest Laboratories, Inc. v. Pillsbury Co.*, 452 F.2d 621 (CA7, 1971) in which a defendant's purchase of assets of a corporation to which a trade secret had been disclosed in confidence was not considered to confer immunity upon the defendant.

When Section 2(b) applies, a court has discretion to substitute an injunction conditioning future use upon payment of a reasonable royalty for an injunction prohibiting future use. Like all injunctive relief for misappropriation, a royalty order injunction is appropriate only if a misappropriator has obtained a competitive advantage through misappropriation and only for the duration of that competitive advantage. In some situations, typically those involving good faith acquirers of trade secrets misappropriated by others, a court may conclude that the same considerations that render a prohibitory injunction against future use inappropriate also render a royalty order injunction inappropriate. See, generally, *Prince Manufacturing, Inc. v. Automatic Partner, Inc.,* 198 USPQ 618 (NJ Super. Ct. 1976) (purchaser of misappropriator's assets from receiver after trade secret disclosed to public through sale of product not subject to liability for misappropriation).

A royalty order injunction under Section 2(b) should be distinguished from a reasonable royalty alternative measure of damages under Section 3(a). See the Comment to Section 3 for discussion of the differences in the remedies.

Section 2(c) authorizes mandatory injunctions requiring that a misappropriator return the fruits of misappropriation to an aggrieved person, e.g., the return of stolen blueprints or the surrender of surreptitious photographs or recordings.

Where more than one person is entitled to trade secret protection with respect to the same information, only that one from whom misappropriation occurred is entitled to a remedy.

SECTION 3. DAMAGES.

(a) In addition to or in lieu of injunctive relief except to the extent that a material and prejudicial change of position prior to acquiring knowledge or reason to know of misappropriation renders a monetary recovery inequitable, a complainant is entitled to recover damages for the actual loss caused by misappropriation. A complainant also may recover for damages that can include both the actual loss caused by misappropriation and the unjust enrichment caused by misappropriation that is not taken into account in computing damages for actual loss. In lieu of damages measured by any other methods, the damages caused by misappropriation may be measured by imposition of liability for a reasonable royalty for a misappropriator's unauthorized disclosure or use of a trade secret.

(b) If willful and malicious misappropriation exists, the court may award exemplary damages in an amount not exceeding twice any award made under subsection (a).

Comment: Like injunctive relief, a monetary recovery for trade secret misappropriation is appropriate only for the period in which information is entitled to protection as a trade secret, plus the additional period, if any, in which a misappropriator retains an advantage over good faith competitors because of misappropriation. Actual damage to a complainant and unjust benefit to a misappropriator are caused by misappropriation during this time alone. See *Conmar Products Corp. v. Universal Slide Fastener Co.*, 172 F.2d 150 (CA2, 1949) (no remedy for period subsequent to disclosure of trade secret by issued patent); *Carboline Co. v. Jarboe*, 454 SW2d 540 (Mo. 1970) (recoverable monetary relief limited to period that it would have taken misappropriator to discover trade secret without misappropriation). A claim for actual damages and net profits can be combined with a claim for injunctive relief, but, if both claims are granted, the injunctive relief ordinarily will preclude a monetary award for a period in which the injunction is effective.

As long as there is no double counting, Section 3(a) adopts the principle of the recent cases allowing recovery of both a complainant's actual losses and a misappropriator's unjust benefit that are caused by misappropriation, e.g., *Tri-Tron International v. Velto*, 525 F.2d 432 (CA9, 1975) (complainant's loss and misappropriator's benefit can be combined). Because certain cases may have sanctioned double counting in a combined award of losses and unjust benefit, e.g., *Telex Corp. v. IBM Corp.*, 510 F.2d 894 (CA10, 1975) (per curiam), cert. dismissed, 423 U.S. 802 (1975) (IBM recovered rentals lost due to displacement by misappropriator's products without deduction for expenses saved by displacement; as a result of rough approximations adopted by the trial judge, IBM also may have recovered developmental costs saved by misappropriator through misappropriation with respect to the same customers), the Act adopts an express prohibition upon the counting of the same item as both a loss to a complainant and an unjust benefit to a misappropriator.

As an alternative to all other methods of measuring damages caused by a misappropriator's past conduct, a complainant can request that damages be based upon a demonstrably reasonable royalty for a misappropriator's unauthorized disclosure or use of a trade secret. In order to justify this alternative measure of damages, there must be competent evidence of the amount of a reasonable royalty.

The reasonable royalty alternative measure of damages for a misappropriator's past conduct under Section 3(a) is readily distinguishable from a Section 2(b) royalty order injunction, which conditions a misappropriator's future ability to use a trade secret upon payment of a reasonable royalty. A Section 2(b) royalty order injunction is appropriate only in exceptional circumstances; whereas a reasonable royalty measure of damages is a general option. Because Section 3(a) damages are awarded for a misappropriator's past conduct and a Section 2(b) royalty order injunction regulates a misappropriator's future conduct, both remedies cannot be awarded for the same conduct. If a royalty order injunction is appropriate because of a person's material and prejudicial change of position prior to having reason to know that a trade secret has been acquired from a misappropriator, damages, moreover, should not be awarded for past conduct that occurred prior to notice that a misappropriated trade secret has been acquired.

Monetary relief can be appropriate whether or not injunctive relief is granted under Section 2. If a person charged with misappropriation has acquired materially and prejudicially changed position in reliance upon knowledge of a trade secret acquired in good faith and without reason to know of its misappropriation by another, however, the same considerations that can justify denial of all injunctive relief also can justify denial of all monetary relief. See *Conmar Products Corp. v. Universal Slide Fastener Co.*, 172 F.2d 1950 (CA2, 1949) (no relief against new employer of employee subject to contractual obligation not to disclose former employer's trade secrets where new employer innocently had committed $40,000 to develop the trade secrets prior to notice of misappropriation).

If willful and malicious misappropriation is found to exist, Section 3(b) authorizes the court to award a complainant exemplary damages in addition to the actual recovery under Section 3(a) an amount not exceeding twice that recovery. This provision follows federal patent law in leaving discretionary trebling to the judge even though there may be a jury; compare 35 U.S.C. Section 284 (1976).

Whenever more than one person is entitled to trade secret protection with respect to the same information, only that one from whom misappropriation occurred is entitled to a remedy.

SECTION 4. ATTORNEY'S FEES. If (i) a claim of misappropriation is made in bad faith, (ii) a motion to terminate an injunction is made or resisted in bad faith, or (iii) willful and malicious misappropriation exists, the court may award reasonable attorney's fees to the prevailing party.

Comment: Section 4 allows a court to award reasonable attorney fees to a prevailing party in specified circumstances as a deterrent to specious claims of misappropriation, to specious efforts by a misappropriator to terminate injunctive relief, and to willful and malicious misappropriation. In the latter situation, the court should take into consideration the extent to which a complainant will recover exemplary damages in determining whether additional attorney's fees should be awarded. Again, patent law is followed in allowing the judge to determine whether attorney's fees should be awarded even if there is a jury; compare 35 U.S.C. Section 285 (1976).

SECTION 5. PRESERVATION OF SECRECY. In an action under this [Act], a court shall preserve the secrecy of an alleged trade secret by reasonable means, which may include granting protective orders in connection with discovery proceedings, holding in-camera hearings, sealing the records of the action, and ordering any person involved in the litigation not to disclose an alleged trade secret without prior court approval.

Comment: If reasonable assurances of maintenance of secrecy could not be given, meritorious trade secret litigation would be chilled. In fashioning safeguards of confidentiality, a court must ensure that a respondent is provided sufficient information to present a defense and a trier of fact sufficient information to resolve the merits. In addition to the illustrative techniques specified in the statute, courts have protected secrecy in these cases by restricting disclosures to a party's counsel and his or her assistants and by appointing a disinterested expert as a special master to hear secret information and report conclusions to the court.

SECTION 6. STATUTE OF LIMITATIONS. An action for misappropriation must be brought within 3 years after the misappropriation is discovered or by the exercise of reasonable diligence should have been discovered. For the purposes of this section, a continuing misappropriation constitutes a single claim.

Comment: There presently is a conflict of authority as to whether trade secret misappropriation is a continuing wrong. Compare *Monolith Portland Midwest Co. v. Kaiser Aluminum & Chemical Corp.*, 407 F.2d 288 (CA9, 1969) (no continuing wrong under California law; limitation period upon all recovery begins upon initial misappropriation) with *Underwater Storage, Inc. v. U. S. Rubber Co.*, 371 F.2d 950 (CADC, 1966), cert. denied; 386 U.S. 911 (1967) (continuing wrong under general principles - limitation period with respect to a specific act of misappropriation begins at the time that the act of misappropriation occurs).

This Act rejects a continuing wrong approach to the statute of limitations but delays the commencement of the limitation period until an aggrieved person discovers or reasonably should have discovered the existence of misappropriation. If objectively reasonable notice of misappropriation exists, three years is sufficient time to vindicate one's legal rights.

SECTION 7. EFFECT ON OTHER LAW.

(a) Except as provided in subsection (b), this [Act] displaces conflicting tort, restitutionary, and other law of this State pertaining to providing civil liability remedies for misappropriation of a trade secret.

(b) This [Act] does not affect:

(1) contractual or other civil liability or relief that is remedies, whether or not based upon misappropriation of a trade secret; or

(2) criminal liability for other civil remedies that are not based upon misappropriation of a trade secret; or

(3) criminal remedies, whether or not based upon misappropriation of a trade secret.

Comment: This act is not a comprehensive remedy does not deal with criminal remedies for trade secret misappropriation and is not a comprehensive statement of civil remedies. It applies to duties imposed by law in order to protect competitively significant secret information that is imposed by law. It does not apply to duties voluntarily assumed through an express or an implied-in-fact contract. The enforceability of covenants not to disclose trade secrets and covenants not to compete that are intended to protect trade secrets, for example, are is governed by other law. The act also does not apply to duties imposed by law that are not dependent upon the existence of competitively significant secret information, like an agent's duty of loyalty to his or her principal.

SECTION 8. UNIFORMITY OF APPLICATION AND CONSTRUCTION. This [Act] shall be applied and construed to effectuate its general purpose to make uniform the law with respect to the subject of this [Act] among states enacting it.

SECTION 9. SHORT TITLE. This [Act] may be cited as the Uniform Trade Secrets Act.

SECTION 10. SEVERABILITY. If any provision of this [Act] or its application to any person or circumstances is held invalid, the invalidity does not affect other provisions or applications of the [Act] which can be given effect without the invalid provision or application, and to this end the provisions of this [Act] are severable.

SECTION 11. TIME OF TAKING EFFECT. This [Act] takes effect on ___, and does not apply to misappropriation occurring prior to the effective date. With respect to a continuing misappropriation that began prior to the effective date, the [Act] also does not apply to the continuing misappropriation that occurs after the effective date.

Comment: The act applies exclusively to misappropriation that begins after its effective date. Neither misappropriation that began and ended before the effective date nor misappropriation that began before the effective date and continued thereafter is subject to the act.

Index